Rockin' the Classics and Classicizin' the Rock

Recent Titles in Discographies

The Blue Note Label: A Discography
Michael Cuscuna and Michel Ruppli, compilers

His Master's Voice/La Voce Del Padrone
Alan Kelly, compiler

Irish Folk Music: A Selected Discography
Deborah L. Schaeffer, compiler

Movie Musicals on Record: A Directory of Recordings of Motion Picture Musicals, 1927-1987
Richard Chigley Lynch, compiler

Classical Music Discographies, 1976-1988: A Bibliography
Michael Gray, compiler

You Got To Be Original, Man!: The Music of Lester Young
Frank Büchmann-Møller

The Decca Hillbilly Discography
Cary Ginell, compiler

Percussion Discography: An International Compilation of Solo and Chamber Percussion Music
Fernando A. Meza, compiler

TV and Studio Cast Musicals on Record: A Discography of Television Musicals and Studio Recordings of Stage and Film Musicals
Richard Chigley Lynch, compiler

Basic Musical Library, "P" Series, 1-1000
Larry F. Kiner and Harry Mackenzie

His Master's Voice/La Voix de Son Maître
Alan Kelly, compiler

Woody Herman: A Guide to the Big Band Recordings, 1936-1987
Dexter Morrill, compiler

The Recorded Performances of Gérard Souzay: A Discography
Manuel Morris, compiler

The Aladdin/Imperial Labels: A Discography
Michel Ruppli, compiler

ROCKIN' THE CLASSICS AND CLASSICIZIN' THE ROCK

A SELECTIVELY ANNOTATED DISCOGRAPHY

First Supplement

Compiled by
Janell R. Duxbury

Discographies, Number 43
MICHAEL GRAY, Series Adviser

GREENWOOD PRESS
New York • Westport, Connecticut • London

Library of Congress Cataloging-in-Publication Data

Duxbury, Janell R.
Rockin' the classics and classicizin' the rock : a selectively annotated discography : first supplement / compiled by Janell R. Duxbury.
p. cm.—(Discographies, ISSN 0192-334X ; no. 43)
Includes bibliographical references and index.
ISBN 0-313-27542-4 (alk. paper)
1. Rock music—Discography. I. Title. II. Series.
ML156.4.R6D9 1985 Suppl.
016.78166'168'0266—dc20 91-7899

British Library Cataloguing in Publication Data is available.

Library of Congress Catalog Card Number: 91-7899
ISBN: 0-313-27542-4
ISSN: 0192-334X

First published in 1991

Greenwood Press, 88 Post Road West, Westport, CT 06881
An imprint of Greenwood Publishing Group, Inc.

Printed in the United States of America

The paper used in this book complies with the Permanent Paper Standard issued by the National Information Standards Organization (Z39.48-1984).

10 9 8 7 6 5 4 3 2 1

To all musicians
who have creatively blended
rock music with classical music
to bridge the gap between them.

Contents

Preface

SCOPE

This selectively annotated discography supplements a previously published volume <u>Rockin' the Classics and Classicizin' the Rock: A Selectively Annotated Discography</u> (1985) which documents the intriguing connections between rock and classical music genres. This Supplement includes both new entries and updates to entries in the earlier work. Both volumes are intended for browsing as well as for researching reference questions. Rock music is an umbrella term used somewhat loosely in this discography to define music with a prominent beat and varying electronic instrumentation. The variants known as early rock and roll, pop rock, progressive rock, reggae, synthesizer music, disco, soul, heavy metal and new wave are encompassed in this definition. The term classical music refers to established works of the major composers spanning the period from the Middle Ages through the Twentieth Century and representing Europe, the United States, and Latin America.

After a revised general historical introduction to the topic of rock and classical connections, several major divisions of new entries follow. Part I, "Rockin' the Classics," details numerous examples of recorded rock instrumentals and songs from the 1950s to the present that borrow musical themes from the classics. The classical essence varies widely from one example to the next. At one extreme are contemporary renditions of complete classical works that do not stray noticeably from the original; at the other extreme are brief classical quotes or phrases, subtly incorporated into rock compositons, which require a very discerning ear. All possible variations between these two extremes are represented in the entries. Part II, "Classicizin' the Rock," details recorded orchestral versions of songs originally composed and/or recorded by rock musicians. Here the musical style varies from strict classical interpretations to pop-style orchestral renditions.

Part III, "Other Connections Between Rock and the Classics," includes a compilation of recordings by rock groups or artists performing with established orchestras and choruses, live performances of rock groups or artists with orchestras before an audience, selected examples of recorded rock which simulate a baroque or classical sound/structure, and examples of the manifest influence of rock on classical music. Part IV, "Update," expands and clarifies the details of specific entries from the 1985 discography. Selected nonrock background examples (e.g., Big Band/Broadway, jazz/new age, parody, and country/folk) are listed in several appendixes. A general index includes the names of classical composers, rock groups, rock artists, orchestras, choruses, orchestra conductors, sound recording producers, and song or instrumental titles.

Although Parts I and II are intended to be as comprehensive as possible, many other examples are still waiting to be discovered or recorded. Part III is selective rather than comprehensive and does not include all possible examples; it highlights those representative of the range of styles and performers which fall into these categories.

This Supplement augments Parts I, II, III and Appendixes of the 1985 discography. Included are new entries which document recently released or recently discovered examples of "rockin' the classics and classicizin' the rock." Updates, expanded detail unknown at the time of the first publication, and minor corrections for the original entries are included in Part IV. New entries also appear in the appendixes.

SOURCES

The best source of information about recorded music is the actual sound recording. When possible, I listened to and looked at recordings from my personal collection and from sound recordings archives, radio station libraries, used record stores, and retail record stores. When the actual recording was unavailable, I consulted numerous music reference books and periodicals. This research in synthesis with my previous research and publication compiles bits and pieces of information from a multitude of sources in order to provide documentation and put it all together in a way which has never been done before.

Information on singles (45 rpm) for this Supplement was obtained from Paul C. Mawhinney's <u>MusicMaster, the 45 RPM Record Directory: 1947 to 1982</u> (1983); Jerry Osborne's <u>Popular & Rock Price Guide for 45's</u> (1981); <u>The Guinness Book of British Hit Singles</u> (1981); Joel Whitburn's <u>Billboard Book of Top 40 Hits, 1955 to Present</u> (1983) and <u>Top Pop, 1955-1982</u> (1983).

Album details for this Supplement were gleaned from Terry Hounsome's New Rock Record (1983); Jerry Osborne's Record Albums (1982); Joel Whitburn's Top Pop Albums, 1955-1985 (1985); Neal Umphred's Rock & Roll Record Albums (1985); Schwann CD Catalog (1985-1989); InMusic (1990-); Phonolog; Music Master (UK); Deutsche Bibliographie: Musiktonträger-Verzeichnis; and Online Computer Library Center (OCLC) union catalog database.

Other information was discovered by researching reviews and articles in Rolling Stone, Melody Maker, Billboard, Variety, Musician, Hi-Fi News & Record Review, and other magazines. In some cases correspondence with recording companies, sound recordings archives, and performers was an effective means of documenting details.

ENTRY FORM

In each of the three major parts and in the update section of this discography the names of groups and the surnames of individual artists are listed alphabetically excluding initial articles. In Parts I, II and III under the heading of each group or artist's name the numbered entries are arranged alphabetically by song/instrumental or album title and followed by relevant discographic details. Entry numbers in Parts I, II and III are preceded by the letter prefix "S" to identify them as supplementary/new entries not included in the 1985 discography. Entry numbers in Part IV, "Update," are listed without a letter prefix and correlate with the entry numbers in the 1985 discography.

In the majority of main entries in Part I each song or instrumental piece (whether from a single or album) is listed according to its respective title. An album title is shown as the main entry when its contents are based primarily on the same classical source or when the titles of its individual selections are repetitive, lengthy, or descriptive of the source information. Part II and Part III also have mixed type entries. Song or instrumental titles are enclosed in quotes (except in content notes) and album titles are underlined. Part IV entries follow similar conventions in an abbreviated format depending on the nature of additions and corrections. The entries include explanations about the placement of these details rather than repeating complete entries.

The order of discographic details follows the same sequence in each entry: song/instrumental and/or album title, year of release, recording company label name, catalog number, and country where released. When a lower case "c" appears before the year in an entry (e.g., c1973, 1974), it first designates the album copyright date and then the year it was released. Single (45 rpm) releases issued in conjunction with an album are listed after the album details. Where possible both United States (US) and United Kingdom (UK) release information is shown. US information is generally listed first and UK, second. Release data for other countries is given only when the recording was originally released outside the US or UK. The term "single" refers to two-selection 7-inch 45 rpm records; "album" refers to multiselection 33 1/3 rpm LPs. The designation "EP" refers to extended play records usually consisting of four to six selections which may be either 45 rpm or 33 1/3 rpm. The term "12-inch single" refers to two-selection 33 1/3 rpm records. The designation "CD" refers to a 4 3/4-inch compact disc played by laser at 500 rpm. CD and audio cassette information is provided in an entry when a recording is available in that format only. Albums (LPs) are often also available in audio cassette and CD formats. When a recording is available in more than one format, only the LP number is listed in the entry. Frequently the numbers for other formats vary only slightly in prefix or suffix except in certain cases when an LP is reissued as a CD with a completely new or different number and/or label. Consult appropriate commercial catalogs for these reissue details.

In Part I the composers and titles of the borrowed classical themes are given as completely as possible. Completeness and specificity of source information varies because certain obscure recordings were not available. Consequently it was occasionally impossible to identify and verify the borrowed classical themes by listening to them. In Part II where the sources of an album's selections are mixed, the names of the rock groups or artists originally performing the pieces are noted in parentheses. In Parts I through IV selective annotations add information such as Billboard pop chart positions, Recording Industry Association of America (RIAA) million seller certifications for singles, Grammy award nominations and winners, album contents, compilation and reissue data, videocassette data, and other facts of interest.

FOR FURTHER READING

Benson, Joe. Uncle Joe's Record Guide: Progressive Rock. Glendale, CA: J. Benson Unlimited, 1989.

Bergman, Billy. Recombinant Do.Re.Mi: Frontiers of the Rock Era. New York: Quill, 1985.

Charlton, Katherine. Rock Music Styles. Dubuque: Wm. C. Brown, 1990.

Curtis, James M. Rock Eras: Interpretations of Music and Society, 1954-1984. Bowling Green, OH: Bowling Green State University Popular Press, 1987.

Doerschuk, Bob. Rock Keyboard. New York: Quill, 1985.

Graves, Barry. "Classic Goes Pop." Musik und Bildung, vol. 5 (April 1973), pp. 181-183.

Greckel, Wil. "Rock and Nineteenth-Century Romanticism: Social and Cultural Parallels." Journal of Musicological Research, vol. 3 (1979), pp. 177-202.

Kneif, Tibor. "Roll Over Beethoven: Zur Beethoven-Rezeption in der Rockmusik." Musik and Bildung, vol. 8 (October 1976), p. 535.

Kozinn, Allan. "The Role of Rock." Symphony, (January/ February 1990), pp. 49-52, 67.

Limbacher, James L. The Song List: A Guide to Contemporary Music From Classical Sources. Ann Arbor: Pierian Press, 1973.

Meltzer, Richard. The Aesthetics of Rock. New York: Something Else Press, 1970 (New York: Da Capo, 1987 reprint).

Miller, Jim. Rolling Stone Illustrated History of Rock & Roll. New York: Rolling Stone Press, 1980 (rev. ed).

Pattison, Robert. The Triumph of Vulgarity: Rock Music in the Mirror of Romanticism. New York: Oxford University Press, 1987.

Rock and the Classics. Minneapolis: University Media Resources, University of Minnesota, 1975 (videorecording).

Schaeffer, John. New Sounds. New York: Harper & Row, 1987.

Schuler, Manfred. "Rockmusik und Kunstmusik der Vergangenheit." Archiv für Musik-Wissenschaft, vol. 35 (1978), pp. 135-150.

Shingler, Joseph J. "Renaissance of Progressive Rock: The Pioneers and the Revivalists." DISCoveries, (June 1990), pp. 30-33.

Stuessy, Joe. Rock and Roll: Its History and Stylistic Development. Englewood Cliffs, NJ: Prentice Hall, 1990.

Weinstein, Robert V. "Rock and Classical: Happy Mixture of Longhairs." Senior Scholastic, (October 31, 1974), pp. 26-27.

Acknowledgments

Most of all I want to again express my appreciation to my parents Ruth and Don and my brother Jon for their patience and untiring research assistance. My mother Ruth assisted with her expert wordprocessing skills. I also want to thank several other people and organizations for their excellent assistance: University of Wisconsin-Madison Mills Music Library; William Schurk, Sound Recordings Archivist, Bowling Green State University, Bowling Green, OH; Consolidated Libraries, North Park College & Theological Seminary, Chicago, IL; Andy Linehan, Popular Music Curator, British Library National Sound Archive, London, England; WORT-FM; Madcity Music Exchange; Wazoo Records; Sugar Shack Record Racks; Half Price Books, Records & Magazines (all of Madison, Wisconsin); Atomic Records (of Milwaukee, Wisconsin); Shelby Singleton Enterprises; Musical Starstreams, syndicated New Age music radio program; Rick Wakeman; Scottish National Ballet; San Francisco Ballet; and Dargason Music. Finally of course, I thank all of the musical artists and groups who produced, performed, and recorded the music in this discography.

Introduction (Revised for Supplement)

At first hearing the average listener may be unaware of the many links between rock music and the classics. One might remember a few examples of "rockin' the classics" and pass them off as interesting anomalies. However the pervasive influence of the classics on rock music has grown from a long line of precedents. Many of the examples noted below are detailed in the 1985 discography and in this Supplement.

Each popular style of music in its day has produced versions of the classics. Many composers throughout music history have delighted in adding a "new" sound to familiar melodies. The range and quality varies widely in these attempts to blend the music of the past with the sound of the present and the future. Nonetheless the classical "hook" draws in the listener with either distinct or vague familiarity. Thus even the early days of ragtime and vaudeville produced their own variations on the classics, though we have few recordings. From the 1920s through the 1940s, James Price Johnson, Jelly Roll Morton, and Fats Waller "jazzed up" the classics, alongside the Big Band versions of Paul Whiteman, Duke Ellington, Harry James, Tommy Dorsey, Glenn Miller, Les Brown, Gene Krupa, Woody Herman, John Kirby, Freddie Martin, and Stan Kenton. James L. Limbacher's <u>The Song List: A Guide to Contemporary Music from Classical Sources</u> (1973) highlights this era of classical borrowing. Many composers of Broadway shows also appropriated classical melodies.

During the 1950s and the 1960s the jazz genre produced "jazzed up" classics by artists such as the Jacques Loussier Trio, Dave Brubeck, and the Swingle Singers. Jazz interpretations continue to the present by artists such as Hubert Laws and Herbie Mann.

There have also been parodies of classical music including those by Spike Jones, Peter Schickele, Anna

Russell, Portsmouth Sinfonia, and Allan Sherman. Even country and folk interpretations of the classics have surfaced from time to time.

Rock versions of the classics began in the early days of rock and roll with the Elegants in 1958, Billy Storm in 1959, and Elvis Presley and Jackie Wilson in 1960. Others followed by producing both rock versions of the classics and the "Classical Rock" sound which imitated the classics (e.g., New York Rock & Roll Ensemble; Left Banke). The Beatles and the Rolling Stones led the way with simulated baroque sounds. This trend continued to grow, culminating in a frenzy of "Baroque Rock" during 1965-1969, peaking in 1967-1968. These years also marked the beginning of the phenomenon of classical musicians performing baroque or classical versions of rock music originally composed and/or performed by rock musicians (e.g., Joshua Rifkin's _The Baroque Beatles Book_).

In fact baroque and rock meshed more successfully than one might expect because both genres share contrapuntal structure and steady rhythmic patterns. A literal meeting of rock and classical instruments occurred about 1966-1967 with the first use of a violin bow on electric guitar as performed by Creation, a British rock group. At the same time, Jimmy Page used that technique in the rock group Yardbirds. He later carried its use into the rock group Led Zeppelin, and in performing with the Firm. Most recently this technique has been used by the rock group Whitesnake to mimic the sound of Led Zeppelin.

The "Classical Rock" or "Art Rock" style grew and matured into the 1970s as it drew on classical style and technique while relying on a rock beat and the use of electric intruments. Through the magic of creative arrangements a mere handful of rock musicians gave forth the lush sounds of a full-blown orchestra. Rock groups which typified this style included: Renaissance; Emerson, Lake & Palmer; Yes; Genesis; and Electric Light Orchestra. This classical influence was also reflected in the recordings of many other rock groups. The "Rock Opera" phenomenon also emerged with the albums _Tommy_ by the Who and _Jesus Christ Superstar_ by Andrew Lloyd-Webber.

Beginning in the late 1960s the development of synthesizers led to their use as substitutes for strings. Ultimately whole orchestras were imitated in the synthesized classics as played by Tomita. Although the use of synthesizers continues to evolve, the inclusion of string sections with rock bands reemerged in the mid-1980s (e.g., China Crisis). This resurgence of an earlier trend shows a continuing dimension in the influence of the classics on rock music. From the late 1970s through the 1980s and into the 1990s, versions of the classics evolved in the styles of disco (e.g., Philarmonics), reggae (e.g., Jah Irie Chorus), heavy metal (e.g., Accept), new wave (e.g., Klaus Nomi; Lords of the New Church), scratch (e.g., Mutant Rockers), and Latin beat (e.g., Latin Rascals). In the late 1980s several rock groups (e.g., Malcolm McLaren; Dollie de Luxe; Kimera) selected opera arias as a popular source of classical borrowing. These developments have taken place in the United States, England and in continental Europe.

Rock versions of the classics have been popular on the Billboard pop singles chart throughout the history of rock music. Walter Murphy's "A Fifth of Beethoven" reached number one on the chart. Number two spots were held by the Toys' "A Lover's Concerto" and Eric Carmen's "All by Myself." Many similar recordings also did very well. Although classical purists might cringe, clearly the record-buying public appreciates these recordings. In assessing the frequency of particular classical themes in popular music, J. S. Bach appears to be the all-time favorite composer. Certain classical themes have been recorded numerous times in a rock style. A good example is Nicolas Rimsky-Korsakov's "Flight of the Bumblebee," recorded in at least sixteen different versions by as many artists.

In a possible attempt to legitimize rock music in the eyes of the nonrock world, rock groups have often performed with established orchestras and choruses or appeared on the same bill with them. These collaborations occur both on sound recordings and in live performances. The most publicly accessible example of this cultural meeting occurred as an NBC network television special on March 14, 1970, entitled "The Switched-on Symphony." The program included appearances by the Los Angeles Philharmonic Orchestra, Jethro Tull, Santana, Nice, Bobby Sherman, Jerry Goodman, Los Angeles Master Chorale, Ray Charles, Christopher Parkening, João Carlos Martins, and Pinchas Zukerman. Beginning in 1980 in Germany, conductor Eberhard Schoener put together an annual "rock-klassik-nacht." Classical and rock performers are included on the same program. For the Grammy Awards telecast of February 25, 1986, rock performer Sting donned a tuxedo and appeared with his rock band and an orchestra. Together they performed his Prokofiev-based song "Russians." On September 13, 1986 Tomita presented a "Back to the Earth" outdoor concert at New York City's Battery Park. He performed his synthesized classics with guest appearances by the choir of the Cathedral Church of St. John the Divine, pianist Nikolai Demidenko, and violinist Mariko Senju. The concert was enhanced by lasers, fireworks and smoke effects. On July 21, 1990 Roger Waters staged a live extravaganza of The Wall in Berlin, Germany which brought numerous guest rock stars together in performance with an orchestra, choir, and a military band.

The Bee Gees toured with a hired orchestra as early as 1968. Emerson, Lake & Palmer tried the same approach for a concert tour in 1977, but it proved to be too expensive and they dropped the orchestra after only fifteen performances. Another strange twist has been the use of tape-recorded or live orchestral introductions just prior to a rock band's appearance on the concert stage. Examples of these efforts to bridge classical and rock genres are: Mott the Hoople (Holst's Jupiter from The Planets); Steve Harley and Cockney Rebel (Ravel/Bolero); David Bowie 1972 tour (Walter Carlos' version of Beethoven/Symphony No. 9, Ode to Joy); Yes (Stravinsky/Firebird); Elvis Presley (R. Strauss/Also Sprach Zarathustra); Rolling Stones (Copland/Fanfare for the Common Man); Queen 1977 tour (Tchaikovsky/1812 Overture); Billy Joel 1986 tour (Gershwin/Rhapsody in Blue).

Rock musicians have also been quick to point out their classical training. Michael Kamen, Dorian Rudnytsky, and Martin Fulterman of New York Rock & Roll Ensemble attended the Julliard School of Music; three members of Electric Light Orchestra were once members of the London Symphony Orchestra; Rick Wakeman of Yes attended the Royal College of Music in London; Annie Lennox of Eurythmics studied for a time at the Royal Academy of Music in London and although she never completed her degree, she was appointed an associate of England's Royal Academy of Music in 1986; Thijs van Leer of Focus attended the Amsterdam Conservatoire; Hans Jürgen Fritz of Triumvirat attended Cologne Conservatory; Ralf Hutter and Florian Schneider of Kraftwerk attended Dusseldorf Conservatory; John Cale attended the Royal Conservatory of Music in London; Joe Jackson attended the Royal Academy of Music in London; and Pat Benatar and Annie Haslam were opera trained. Various members of Ars Nova, Mothers of Invention, and First Edition also had classical training.

There is evidence that the classical world has also taken notice of the rock world. Leonard Bernstein has been quoted in praise of the New York Rock & Roll Ensemble, the Beatles, and the Who's Tommy, the rock opera which earned the distinction of playing the Met and other opera houses. Since the Henry Wood Promenade concerts began in 1895, the first rock group to ever appear at the London Proms was Soft Machine at Royal Albert Hall on August 13, 1970. Pink Floyd was the first rock group to perform at the Montreux Classical Music Festival on September 18, 1971. Emerson, Lake & Palmer's Works, Volume 1 was reviewed in the classical, rather than the rock, section of Stereo Review. Both established orchestras (e.g., the London Symphony Orchestra) and pop-style orchestras (e.g., 101 Strings) have recorded their own quasi-classical orchestral arrangements of rock music originally composed and/or recorded by rock musicians. Examples of "classicizin' the rock" show an array of Beatles' compositions as the most popular choice for this blend of the new with the old. In a double twist the Royal Philharmonic Orchestra recorded disco versions of the classics in the Hooked on Classics series which was popular and sold strongly. Orchestras have used other rock trappings for their "straight" versions of the classics. Some symphony orchestras have added rock-style laser and light shows to their concerts. Performers such as Virgil Fox and his "heavy organ" arrangements of J.S. Bach used light shows in rock venues (e.g., Winterland at San Francisco) as well as in "legitimate" venues (e.g., Carnegie Hall).

The packaging of classical albums has, at times, imitated that of rock albums. In the period between 1969 and 1973 both Columbia and RCA Red Seal released "Greatest Hits" albums by most of the major classical composers. Columbia's Greatest Hits of 1720, ...1721, and ...1790 featured album covers with Billboard-like pop charts listing the contents. London Records' Orphic Egg composer series chose unconventional album titles (e.g., Bach's Head, Ravel's Head, etc.) for at least eight different classical composers. Although the versions of these composers' music were "straight," rock critics supplied hip street-talk liner notes for some, and artists created psychedelic album covers. In a parallel manner artists have reproduced works of great art intact or in altered form on scattered rock album covers. In contrast to Walter Carlos' Switched-on Bach, Columbia also released Switched-off Bach, which featured straight versions of the same pieces used on Carlos' synthesizer album. Compilations of straight versions of classical pieces once used for rock interpretations were released by Columbia (Joy! The Great Composers' Hits for the '70s) and RCA Red Seal (Heavy Hits: Great Music That Inspired Today's Hits and Joy: Great Classics That Inspired Great Pop and Rock Hits of the '60s and '70s). In 1978, the Philadelphia Orchestra employed rock star David Bowie as a narrator on a recording of Peter and the Wolf. The first rock-style picture-disc of classical music appeared in 1979 in France as Front Populaire, featuring various classical orchestras.

The most recent manifestations of rock influences on classical music are classical videos such as "Girls Talk" by Linda Nardini on piano and the "Amadeus" (1985) video which pairs Wolfgang Amadeus Mozart's "Symphony no. 25 in G Minor" with alternating clips from the motion picture film Amadeus and from rock videos. The Rochester (New York) Philharmonic Orchestra produced a classical video using rock-like images and editing for Hector Berlioz's "March to the Scaffold." There are plans for future productions of Sergei Prokofiev's "Lieutenant Kije Suite" and Claude Debussy's "Prelude to the Afternoon of a Faun."

Present day classical composers have been slow to admit the influence of rock music on their compositions. One exception is Hans Werner Henze, who mentioned that he was inspired by the Rolling Stones for his 1968 secular cantata Musen Siziliens. Avant-garde experimental composers such as Philip Glass and Glenn Branca have integrated rock rhythm, repetition, and heavy amplification in their works. Philip Glass released rock-style videos of sections of his album The Photographer. Glass also produced several rock albums and scored portions of a rock song (see Supplement, Part IIID4). Classical performers and conductors have also contributed to rock music albums.

A final note involves some controversy over rock versions of the classics. Added to the scorn of classical purists is the furor over failure to give credit to the classical composers. Some rock groups are very scrupulous about this courtesy while others do not give credit at all. When Emerson, Lake & Palmer failed to acknowledge Béla Bartók and Leos Janácek on their first album, several magazine articles denounced this omission. Their later albums usually acknowledged their sources and they added Janácek to the credits of their 1979 live album version of "Knife-Edge," which appeared originally on their first album.

In England, the controversy has been more prominent because the British Broadcasting Corporation (BBC) has from time to time banned tunes lifted from the classics. In fact Tomita's 1976 album <u>The Planets</u> was actually banned for sale and use in the United Kingdom after a 1977 court injunction was awarded to Gustav Holst's daughter. She objected to the synthesizer version of her father's composition. This album is available outside England.

Whether used for reference and research or for browsing, the following Supplement to the author's 1985 discography identifies and documents more examples and further details of the fascinating profusion of connections between rock and classical music genres.

Rockin' the Classics and Classicizin' the Rock

I.

Rockin' the Classics

ACCEPT

S001 "Metal heart." Metal heart. 1985 Portrait BFR-39974, US/ 1985 Portrait PRT-26358, UK.

Source: Tchaikovsky/Marche slave, op. 31; Beethoven/ Für Elise
Note: The Tchaikovsky theme is used in the introduction and the Beethoven theme is performed as a guitar solo in this heavy metal piece. This song also appears on the live EP Kaizoku-ban (1985 Portrait 5R-401261, US/ 1985 Portrait PRT-54916, UK).

ALLIGATOR

S002 "Hall of the mountain king." Alligator (featuring Leslie West). 1989 IRS IRS-82016, US/ 1989 IRS EIRSA-1017, UK.

Source: Grieg/Peer Gynt suite no. 1, op. 46, mvt. 4 (In the hall of the mountain king)
Note: Leslie West is the leader of this rock band.

APOLLO 100

S003 "Grand march/Aida." Classical gas. 1981 Music for Pleasure MFP-50526, UK.

Source: Verdi/Aida, Grand march

S004 "Intermezzo cavalleria rusticana." Classical gas. 1981 Music for Pleasure MFP-50526, UK.

Source: Mascagni/Cavalleria rusticana, intermezzo

S005 "Là ci darem las mano/Don Giovanni." Classical gas. 1981 Music for Pleasure MFP-50526, UK.

Source: Mozart/Don Giovanni, Là ci darem la mano

S006 "Overture light cavalry." Classical gas. 1981 Music for Pleasure MFP-50526, UK.

Source: von Suppé/Light cavalry overture

S007 "Overture to the marriage of Figaro." Classical gas. 1981 Music for Pleasure MFP-50526, UK.

Source: Mozart/Marriage of Figaro overture

S008 "Slaves chorus Nabucco." Classical gas. 1981 Music for Pleasure MFP-50526, UK.

Source: Verdi/Nabucco, Slaves chorus

S009 "La Traviata." Classical gas. 1981 Music for Pleasure MFP-50526, UK.

Source: Verdi/La Traviata, Act I, prelude

B. BUMBLE AND THE STINGERS

S010 "Rockin'-on-'n'-off/Mashed #5." 1962 Rendezvous 174, US (single).

Source: Rachmaninoff; Beethoven

BAKER, JEFFREY REID

S011 Carmina burana. 199? release pending.

Source: Orff/Carmina burana

S012 Everyone's favorite synthesizer pieces. 1989 Newport Classic NCD-60114, US (CD).

Source: as listed below
Contents: Beethoven/Für Elise -- Mozart and Beethoven/Turkish march medley -- Gounod (J. S. Bach)/Ave Maria -- Sinding/Rustles of spring -- MacDowell/To a wild rose -- de Falla/Ritual fire dance -- Ravel/Pavane pour une Infante defunte -- Brahms/Hungarian dance no. 5 -- Chaminade/The flatterer -- Ellmenreich/Spinning song -- Satie/Gymnopedie no. 1 -- Gottschalk/Banjo -- Boccherini/Minuet -- MacDowell/Shadow dance -- Liszt/Liebestraüme -- Ravel/Waltz (in the style of Borodin) -- Moszkowski/Guitarre -- Mendelssohn/Spinning song -- Debussy/Reverie -- Chopin/Minute waltz -- Rachmaninoff/Prelude in C# minor -- Rimsky-Korsakov/Flight of the bumblebee -- Mendelssohn/Rondo capriccioso -- Schumann/Traumerei -- Prokofiev/March from the Love of three oranges

S013 Lisztronique. 1987 Newport Classic NC-30022 (cassette), NC-60022 (CD), US.

Source: Liszt/as listed below
Relevant contents: Piano concerto no. 1 in E flat -- La campanella/"The bells" (Grandes études de Paganini, no. 3) -- Beside a spring/Au bord d'une source (Années de pèlerinage, première année, no. 4) -- Un sospiro/"A sigh" (Études de concert, no. 3) -- Gnomenreigen/Dance of the gnomes -- Hungarian rhapsody no. 2 -- Totentanz
Note: This is recital of Liszt works performed on synthesizer.

S014 Rhapsody in electric blue. 1987 Newport Classic NC-30042 (cassette), NC-60042 (CD), US.

Source: Gershwin/as listed below
Relevant Contents: Rhapsody in blue -- Three preludes: Allegro ben ritmato e deciso, Andante con moto e poco rubato, Allegro ben ritmato e deciso -- An American in Paris -- Concerto in F: Allegro, Adagio, Allegro agitato
Note: This album features synthesizer realizations of Gershwin works.

BEATLES

S015 "The barber of Seville." Strawberry Fields forever. 198? Nems CLUE-9, UK (bootleg LP).

Source: Rossini/Barber of Seville
Note: The Beatles perform a vocalese version of a familiar theme from this opera accompanied by an orchestra recording. This album is also available with the title Now or never (198? AT-88E [bootleg LP]).

S016 "Not a second time." Meet the Beatles!. 1964 Capitol T-2047 (mono), ST-2047 (stereo), US/ With the Beatles. 1963 Parlophone PMC-1206 (mono), PCS-3045 (stereo), UK.

Source: Mahler/The song of the earth (Das lied von der erde)
Note: The Aeolian cadence at the end of this Beatles' song is identical to the progression at the end of Mahler's piece.

S017 "September song." 1960 unreleased.

Source: Weill/Knickerbocker holiday, September song
Note: Ringo Starr was drummer in a backing group for Lu Walters (real name Walter Eymond) of Rory Storm and the Hurricanes. The song was recorded October 15, 1960 in Germany.

S018 "She loves you." The Beatles second album. 1964 Capitol T-2080 (mono), ST-2080 (stereo), US (album); 1963 Swan 4152, US/ 1963 Parlophone R-5055, UK (singles).

Source: Bach/Goldberg variations, BWV 988, quodlibet
Note: This song's melody is somewhat similar to one of the tunes in the quodlibet at the end of Bach's variations. This Beatles' song reached #1 on the Billboard pop singles chart. The song is also included on the EP Beatles million sellers (1965 Parlophone GEP-8946, UK) and the albums A collection of oldies (1966 Parlophone PCS-7016, UK), The Beatles 1962-1966 (1973 Apple [Capitol] SKBO-3403, US/ 1973 Apple PCSP-717, UK), The Beatles at the Hollywood Bowl (1977 Capitol SMAS-11638, US/ 1977 EMI EMTV-4, UK), and 20 greatest hits (1982 Capitol SV-12245, US/ 1982 Parlophone PCTC-260, UK).

S019 "Summertime." 1960 unreleased.

Source: Gershwin/Porgy and Bess, Summertime
Note: John Lennon, Paul McCartney, George Harrison, Stu Sutcliffe and Ringo Starr (subbing for Pete Best) recorded this song as a backing group for Lu Walters (real name Walter Eymond) of Rory Storm and the Hurricanes. The song was recorded on October 15, 1960 in Germany.

BECK, JEFF

S020 "Where were you." Jeff Beck's guitar shop. 1989 Epic OE-44313-1, US/ 1989 Epic EPC-463472, UK.

Source: Vivaldi/Concerto no. 2 in D, mvt. 2
Note: This song is reminiscent of Vivaldi's piece and sounds like a classical symphony.

BEGGAR'S OPERA

S021 "Light cavalry." Act one. 1971 Verve V6-5080, US/ 1971 Vertigo 6360-018, UK.

Source: von Suppé/Light cavalry overture

S022 "Poet and peasant." Act one. 1971 Verve V6-5080, US/ 1971 Vertigo 6360-018, UK.

Source: von Suppé/Poet and peasant overture

BENNINGHOFF'S BAD ROCK BLUES BAND

S023 "Etude - op. 10 #3, parts 1 and 2." Evening with Chopin. 1976 Plantation PLP-502, US.

Source: Chopin/Etude in E, op. 10, no. 3

S024 "Fantaisie-impromptu - op. 66." _Evening with Chopin_. 1976 Plantation PLP-502, US.

Source: Chopin/Fantaisie impromptu, op. 66

S025 "Here comes the night." _Evening with Chopin_. 1976 Plantation PLP-502, US.

Source: Chopin/Nocturne in E flat major, op. 9, no. 2
Note: The Chopin theme is used as a brief interlude.

S026 "In-stra-mental." _Evening with Chopin_. 1976 Plantation PLP-502, US.

Source: Chopin/Waltz, op. 64, no. 2

S027 "Instri-sancti." _Evening with Chopin_. 1976 Plantation PLP-502, US.

Source: Chopin/Etude in E, op. 10, no. 3

S028 "Prelude in A major - op. 28 #7, part 1 and part 2." _Evening with Chopin_. 1976 Plantation PLP-502, US.

Source: Chopin/Prelude in A major, op. 28, no. 7

S029 "Prelude in A minor - op. 28 #2." _Evening with Chopin_. 1976 Plantation PLP-502, US.

Source: Chopin/Prelude in A minor, op. 28, no. 2

S030 "Prelude in C minor - op. 28 #20." _Evening with Chopin_. 1976 Plantation PLP-502, US.

Source: Chopin/Prelude in C minor, op. 28, no. 20

S031 "Prelude in E minor - op. 28 #4." _Evening with Chopin_. 1976 Plantation PLP-502, US.

Source: Chopin/Prelude in E minor, op. 28, no. 4

S032 "Waltz - op. 64 #2, parts 1, 2 and 3." _Evening with Chopin_. 1976 Plantation PLP-502, US.

Source: Chopin/Waltz, op. 64, no. 2

BEYOND THE PLANETS

S033 _Beyond the planets_. 1986 Telstar STAR-2244, UK.

Source: Holst/The planets, op. 32
Contents: Waves -- The journey -- Mars, the bringer of war -- Venus, the bringer of peace -- Mercury, the winged messenger -- Jupiter, the bringer of jollity -- Circles -- Saturn, the bringer of old age --

Uranus, the magician -- Neptune, the mystic -- The heavens reply -- Beyond
Note: This interpretation is performed by Kevin Peek from the rock group Sky, Rick Wakeman and Jeff Wayne. The narration is by Patrick Allen.

BIRDSONGS OF THE MESOZOIC

S034 "The rite of spring (excerpts)." Magnetic flip. 1984 Ace of Hearts AHS-10018, US.

Source: Stravinsky/The rite of spring
Note: This instrumental also appears on the compilation Sonic geology (1988 Rykodisc RCD-20073, US [CD]).

BLEY, CARLA

S035 "Lost in the stars." Lost in the stars: the music of Kurt Weill. 1985 A&M SP9-5104, US/ 1985 A&M AMA-5104, UK.

Source: Weill/Lost in the stars, Lost in the stars
Note: Carla Bley performed with Phil Woods on this recording.

BOWIE, DAVID

S036 "Alabama song." 1980 RCA BOW-5, UK (single).

Source: Weill/The rise and fall of the city of Mahagonny, Alabama song
Note: This is a studio version of a song featured during Bowie's 1978 world tour. It also appears as a B-side of the single "Crystal Japan" (1980 RCA SS-3270, Japan). Live versions appear on Live in Stockholm 1979 (1979 Audifon, Germany) and 1978 bootleg albums Forever yours, Kiss you in the rain, and Speed of life.

BOYD, LIONA

S037 "Memories of a thousand moons." Persona. 1986 CBS FM-42120, US and UK.

Source: Tárrega/Recuerdos de la Alhambra

S038 "Sea of tranquility." Persona. 1986 CBS FM-42120, US and UK.

Source: Brahms
Note: This pop rendition of Brahms was adapted and arranged for guitar, piano, steel string guitar, bass strings and drums by Michael Kamen who also performs on piano keyboards and bass strings. Kamen was formerly a member of New York Rock and Roll Ensemble.

BRAGG, BILLY

S039 "Blake's Jerusalem." The Internationale. 1990 Elektra/Utility 60960-2, US (CD)/ 1990 Utility UTIL-11, UK (CD).

Source: Parry/Jerusalem
Note: Bragg's vocal solo features piano and backup singers in a nearly traditional rendition.

BUCKINGHAM, LINDSEY

S040 "September song." Law and order. 1981 Asylum 5E-561, US/ 1981 Mercury 6302-167, UK.

Source: Weill/Knickerbocker holiday, September song

BUTLER, RICHARD

S041 "Alabama song." Lost in the stars: the music of Kurt Weill. 1985 A&M SP9-5104, US/ 1985 A&M AMA-5104, UK.

Source: Weill/The rise and fall of the city of Mahagonny, Alabama song
Note: Richard Butler of Psychedelic Furs performs with Ralph Schuckett on this recording.

CAMARATA CONTEMPORARY CHAMBER GROUP/ORCHESTRA

S042 The electronic spirit of Erik Satie. 1972 Deram DES-18066, US.

Source: Satie/as listed below
Contents: Chapitres tournes en tous: Celle qui parle trop/Le porteur de grosses pierres/Regrets des enfermés (Jonas et Latude) -- Croquis et agaceries d'un bonhomme en bois: Tyrolienne turque/Danse maigre (à la manière de des Messieurs)/Españana -- Reverie de l'enfance de Pantagruel/Jeux de Gargantua -- Preludes flasques (pour un chien): Voix d'intérieur/Chanson canine/Avec camaraderie -- Les trois valses distinguées du précieux dégoûté: Sa taille/Son binocle/Ses jambes -- Cinq grimaces pour le songe -- Sports & divertissements
Note: The music on this album is arranged by Salvador Camarata for moog synthesizer and instrumental ensemble.

S043 "Heures séculaires et instantanées: Crépuscule matinal." The velvet gentleman: the music of Erik Satie. 1970 Deram DES-18036, US.

Source: Satie/Heures séculaires et instantanées: Crépuscule matinal
Note: The Camarata Contemporary Chamber Group

includes flute, oboe, clarinet and guitar. On this piece they are joined by moog synthesizer and orchestra. This album was reissued (1983 London Jubilee JL-41063, UK).

CARLOS, WENDY

S044 Peter and the wolf/Carnival of the animals - part II. 1988 CBS FM-44567, US.

Source: Prokofiev/Peter and the wolf, op. 67; Saint-Saëns/Carnaval des animaux
Note: Music on this album was arranged and performed on synthesizer by Wendy Carlos. "Weird Al" Yankovic narrates. "Carnival of the animals - part II" is an original piece inspired by the Saint-Saëns work.

CARMEN, ERIC

S045 "Never gonna fall in love again." Eric Carmen. 1975 Arista AL-4057, US/ 1976 Arista ARTY-120, UK (albums); 1976 Arista 0184, US/ 1976 Arista , UK (singles).

Source: Rachmaninoff/Symphony no. 2 in E minor, op. 27, mvt. 3, introduction
Note: The single reached #11 on the Billboard pop singles chart. This is one of at least three pieces on the album which is based on a Rachmaninoff theme. Two others are described in the 1985 discography of Rockin' the Classics and Classicizin' the Rock. "Never gonna fall in love again" also appears on the compilation The best of Eric Carmen (1988 Arista AL-8547, US/ 1989 Arista 20899, UK).

CELTIC FROST

S046 "Danse macabre." Morbid tales. 1985 Metal Blade/ Enigma 72016-1, US/ 1987 Noise N-0017, UK/ 1984 Noise N-0017, Germany.

Source: Saint-Saëns/Danse macabre, op. 40
Note: Although this instrumental does not borrow the actual melody of the original, it takes its title and general milieu.

COLEMAN, CY

S047 "Dance in tangerine." The ages of rock: Cy Coleman plays the classic beat. 196? MGM SE-4502, US.

Source: Grieg/Peer Gynt suite no. 1, op. 46, mvt. 3, first theme (Anitra's dance)

S048 "Fugue in white." The ages of rock: Cy Coleman plays the classic beat. 196? MGM SE-4502, US.

Source: J. S. Bach/Well-tempered clavier, book I, fugue no. 16 in G minor

S049 "Pavanne in purple." The ages of rock: Cy Coleman plays the classic beat. 196? MGM SE-4502, US.

Source: Ravel/Pavane for a dead princess

S050 "Prelude in black." The ages of rock: Cy Coleman plays the classic beat. 196? MGM SE-4502, US.

Source: Rachmaninoff/Prelude in C sharp minor, op. 3, no. 2

S051 "Prelude in blue." The ages of rock: Cy Coleman plays the classic beat. 196? MGM SE-4502, US.

Source: Chopin/Prelude in E minor, op. 28, no. 4

S052 "Prelude in ivory." The ages of rock: Cy Coleman plays the classic beat. 196? MGM SE-4502, US.

Source: J. S. Bach/Well-tempered clavier, book I, prelude no. 1

S053 "Reverie in topaz." The ages of rock: Cy Coleman plays the classic beat. 196? MGM SE-4502, US.

Source: Debussy/Rêverie

S054 "Rhapsody in red." The ages of rock: Cy Coleman plays the classic beat. 196? MGM SE-4502, US.

Source: Liszt/Hungarian rhapsody no. 2 in C sharp minor

S055 "Rondo in lemon yellow." The ages of rock: Cy Coleman plays the classic beat. 196? MGM SE-4502, US.

Source: Mozart/Piano sonata no. 11 in A major, K. 300i (331), mvt. 3 (Rondo alla turca)

S056 "Sonata in shocking pink." The ages of rock: Cy Coleman plays the classic beat. 196? MGM SE-4502, US.

Source: Mozart/Sonata no. 3 in C major, K. 545

S057 "Waltz in lime." The ages of rock: Cy Coleman plays the classic beat. 196? MGM SE-4502, US.

Source: Chopin/Waltz in E minor

COLLINS, JUDY

S058 "A ballata of Francesco Landini." Wildflowers. 1968 Elektra EKS-74012, US/ 1971 Elektra K-42014, UK.

Source: Landini/Ballata

S059 "Jerusalem." Trust your heart. 1987 Gold Castle 171-002-1, US/ 1987 Gold Castle/Virgin VGC-7, UK.

Source: Parry/Jerusalem

COOKE, SAM

S060 "Goin' home." Sam Cooke. 1961 RCA LPM-2293, US.

Source: Dvorák/Symphony no. 9 (old no. 5) in E minor (from the New World), op. 95, mvt. 2 (largo)

CREACH, PAPA JOHN

S061 "Silver bird." Inphasion. 1978 DJM DJM-18, US/ 1978 DJM DJF-20545, UK.

Source: Brahms

CROSS, TIM

S062 Classic landscsape. 1986 Coda NAGE-3, US and UK.

Relevant Contents: Excerpt from the Matthew passion: "Kommt, Ihr tochter, Helft mir klagen" (J. S. Bach) -- Symphony no. 41 in C major K. 551: Jupiter 3rd movement (Mozart) -- Piano concerto no. 4 in G major opus 58: 2nd movement (Beethoven) -- Brandenburg concerto no. 4 in G major (J. S. Bach) -- An die musik, op. 88, no. 4 (Schubert) -- Enigma variation no. 9 "Nimrod" (Elgar)
Note: This album features mostly electronic arrangements of the classics. "Brandenburg concerto no. 4 in G major" is also on the compilation album Standing stones (1986 Coda NAGE-5, US and UK).

CURVED AIR

S063 "Everdance/Bright summer's day '68/Piece of mind." Second album. 1971 Warner Bros. WS-1951, US/ 1971 Warner Bros. K-46092, UK.

Source: Beethoven/Symphony no. 6 in F, op. 68 (Pastoral)

CUSCO

S064 "Air." Concierto de Aranjuez. 1986 CBS/Sony 32DP-456, Japan (CD)/ 1989 Prudence 572-17463-CL, Germany (CD).

Source: J. S. Bach/Suite no. 3 in D major for orchestra, BWV 1068, Air for the G string
Note: This German group incorporates synthesizer, guitar, bass and drums.

S065 "Ave Maria." Concierto de Aranjuez. 1986 CBS/Sony 32DP-456, Japan (CD)/ 1989 Prudence 572-17463-CL, Germany (CD).

Source: Gounod (J. S. Bach)/Ave Maria

S066 "Concierto de Aranjuez." Concierto de Aranjuez. 1986 CBS/Sony 32DP-456, Japan (CD)/ 1989 Prudence 572-17463-CL, Germany (CD).

Source: Rodrigo/Concierto de Aranjuez

S067 "Largo." Concierto de Aranjuez. 1986 CBS/Sony 32DP-456, Japan (CD)/ 1989 Prudence 572-17463-CL, Germany (CD).

Source: Handel/Largo

S068 "Menuett." Concierto de Aranjuez. 1986 CBS/Sony 32DP-456, Japan (CD)/ 1989 Prudence 572-17463-CL, Germany (CD).

Source: Boccherini/Quintet in E, mvt. 3, first theme

S069 "Mondscheinsonate." Concierto de Aranjuez. 1986 CBS/Sony 32DP-456, Japan (CD)/ 1989 Prudence 572-17463-CL, Germany (CD).

Source: Beethoven/Sonata no. 14 in C sharp minor, op. 27, no. 2 (Moonlight sonata)

S070 "Neue welt symphonie." Concierto de Aranjuez. 1986 CBS/Sony 32DP-456, Japan (CD)/ 1989 Prudence 572-17463-CL, Germany (CD).

Source: Dvorák/Symphony no. 9 (old no. 5) in E minor (from the New World), op. 95

S071 "Pastorale." Apurimac. 1988 Higher Octave HOMCD-7016, US (CD)/ 1985 CBS/Sony 32DP-220, Japan (CD)/ 1989 Prudence 572-17023-CY, Germany (CD).

Source: Bach ?

S072 "Peer Gynt-suite." Concierto de Aranjuez. 1986 CBS/Sony 32DP-456, Japan (CD)/ 1989 Prudence 572-17463-CL, Germany (CD).

Source: Grieg/Peer Gynt suite

S073 "Recuerdos de la Alhambra." Concierto de Aranjuez. 1986 CBS/Sony 32DP-456, Japan (CD)/ 1989 Prudence 572-17463-CL, Germany (CD).

Source: Tárrega/Recuerdos de la Alhambra

S074 "Schwanensee-Nussknacker." Concierto de Aranjuez. 1986 CBS/Sony 32DP-456, Japan (CD).

Source: Tchaikovsky/Swan Lake suite and Nutcracker suite

S075 "Sonate in A-dur." Concierto de Aranjuez. 1986 CBS/Sony 32DP-456, Japan (CD)/ 1989 Prudence 572-17463-CL, Germany (CD).

Source: Mozart/Piano sonata no. 11 in A major, K. 300i (331)

DARIN, BOBBY

S076 "Mack the knife." That's all. 1959 Atco SD33-104, US/ 1959 London HAE-2172 (mono), UK (albums); 1959 Atlantic 13056; Atco 45-6147, US/ 1959 London HLE-8939, UK (singles).

Source: Weill/The threepenny opera, Moritat (Mack the knife)
Note: This song also appears on Darin at the Copa (196? Atco SD33-122, US/ 1960 London HAE-2291 [mono], SAH-6103 [stereo], UK) and on the compilation Darin 1936-1973 (1974 Motown M813V1, US/ 1982 Motown STMS-5062, UK).

DEEP PURPLE

S077 "Knocking at your back door." Nobody's perfect. 1988 Mercury 835-897-1, US/ 1988 Polydor PODV-10, UK.

Source: Beethoven/Für Elise
Note: The Beethoven theme is part of a medley which opens this live recording of the song.

S078 "Under the gun." Perfect strangers. 1984 Mercury 422-824-003-1-M-1, US/ 1985 Polydor POLH-16, UK.

Source: Elgar/Pomp and circumstance, op. 39, no. 1, 2nd theme
Note: Seven measures of the Elgar theme emerge in the middle of this Deep Purple song.

DEODATO (Eumir Deodato)

S079 "Ave Maria." Whirlwinds. 1974 MCA MCA-410, US/ 1974 MCA MCG-3518, UK.

Source: Schubert/Ave Maria (op. 52, no. 6)

DOLBY, THOMAS

S080 "Fragment." Musical offerings to the spirit of Bach. 1985 Keyboard Soundpage (March 1985), US.

Source: J. S. Bach/Suite no. 2 in D minor, BWV 1008, Menuet no. 2 and Menuet no. 1
Note: Using sampling of a cellist recording, Dolby synthesizes a short piece on a Fairlight CMI.

DOLLIE DE LUXE

S081 "Carmen/Gimme some lovin'." Rock vs. opera. 1987 A&M SP-9131, US ?/ 1986 Spartan SPLP-006, UK/ 1985 Notabene NBLP-104, Norway (albums); 1986 Spartan SP-138, UK (7" single); 1986 Spartan 12SP-138, UK (12" single).

Source: Bizet/Carmen, Habañera (& Spencer Davis Group/Gimme some lovin')
Note: This recording features opera sung to a rock beat with pop/rock tunes and lyrics layered over. Vocals performed by this Norwegian rock group are accompanied by guitar, bass guitar, drums and percussion.

S082 "Caro nome/Sex & drugs & rock & roll." Rock vs. opera. 1987 A&M SP-9131, US ?/ 1986 Spartan SPLP-006, UK/ 1985 Notabene NBLP-104, Norway.

Source: Verdi/Rigoletto, Caro nome (Gilda's aria) (& Ian Dury/Sex & drugs & rock & roll)

S083 "The magic flute (Beatles mix)." Rock vs. opera. 1987 A&M SP-9131, US ?/ 1986 Spartan SPLP-006, UK/ 1985 Notabene NBLP-104, Norway.

Source: Mozart/The magic flute: Overture, Zum Leiden, Du du du, O Isis und Osiris, Der Hölle Rache, Ach Ich fühl's, Ein Mädchen oder Weibchen, Finale (& Beatles/A hard day's night, Taxman, Paperback writer, Daytripper, You won't see me, I am the walrus, Because, Helter skelter, Get back, Mean Mr. Mustard, A day in the life, Lucy in the sky with diamonds, For no one, Eleanor Rigby, She's leaving home, Lady Madonna, All you need is love)

S084 "Queen of the night/Satisfaction." Rock vs. opera. 1987 A&M SP-9131, US ?/ 1986 Spartan SPLP-006, UK/ 1985 Notabene NBLP-104, Norway.

Source: Mozart/The magic flute, Der Hölle Rache (Queen of the night aria) (& Rolling Stones/ Satisfaction)

S085 "Vilja/Whatever you want." Rock vs. opera. 1987 A&M SP-9131, US ?/ 1986 Spartan SPLP-006, UK/ 1985 Notabene NBLP-104, Norway.

Source: Lehár/The merry widow, Vilja
(& Status Quo/Whatever you want)

S086 "The waltz arias." Rock vs. opera. 1987 A&M SP-1 31, US ?/ 1986 Spartan SPLP-006, UK/ 1985 Notabene NBLP-104, Norway.

Source: Offenbach/Tales of Hoffmann, Schöne Nacht du Liebesnacht (Lovely night); Puccini/Gianni Schicchi, O mio babbino caro; J. Strauss, Jr./Die Fledermaus, Adele's couplet; Gounod/Romeo and Juliet, Valsette (Waltz song); Gounod/Faust, Ah! Je ris (The jewel song); Puccini/Madame Butterfly, Un bel di vedremo

DOORS

S087 "Adagio." An American prayer. 1978 Elektra 5E-502, US/ 1978 Elektra K-52111, UK.

Source: Albinoni/Adagio in G minor for strings and organ
Note: This piece appears at the end of the album. It is also on the videocassette Dance on fire (1985 MCA Home Video VHS-80157, US).

S088 "Alabama song." The Doors. 1967 Elektra EKS-74007, US and UK.

Source: Weill/The rise and fall of the city of Mahagonny, Alabama song
Note: This song is also part of a medley on the live album Absolutely live! (1970 Elektra EKS-2-9002, US/ 1971 Elektra K-62005, UK). Another live version from 1968 appears on the videocassette Live at the Hollywood Bowl (1987 MCA Home Video VHS-80592, US). A rare live version of "Alabama song" preceded by a few lines from "Mack the knife" (another Weill song) appears on the French fan club album Resurrection (1971 Paris Records [no number], France).

DORSEY, DON

S089 Bachbusters. 1985 Telarc DG-10123, US.

Source: J. S. Bach/as listed below
Contents: Italian concerto, BWV 971 -- Two and three part inventions nos. 1, 8, 10, 12, 15 -- Diverse kanons, BWV 1087 -- Toccata and fugue in D minor, BWV 565 -- Cantata no. 147: Jesu, joy of man's desiring, BWV 147
Note: This music of J. S. Bach is recorded on digital and other authentic period synthesizers.

S090 Beethoven or bust. 1988 Telarc CD-80153, US (CD).

Source: Beethoven/as listed below
Contents: "Rage over a lost penny," Rondo a capriccio in G major, op. 129 -- Mixed bagatelles (op. 33) -- "Moonlight" sonata -- Various variations (from 15 "Eroica" variations, op. 35) -- Presto from Sonata no. 6 -- Six ecossaises -- Für Elise (Albumblatt) -- Scherzo: Allegro vivace from sonata no. 18 ("Western") -- Ode to Ludwig (based on Ode to joy from Symphony no. 9)
Note: This album features synthesizer versions of Beethoven works.

ELECTRIC LIGHT ORCHESTRA

S091 "Fire on high." Face the music. 1975 United Artists UA-LA546-G, US/ 1975 Jet LP-11, UK.

Source: Handel/Messiah, Hallelujah chorus
Note: The introductory sequence of this song includes a few measures of the Handel piece. The album was reissued (1978 Jet JZ-35527, US/ 1978 Jet LP-201, UK).

S092 "Mr. Radio." Electric Light Orchestra. 1971 United Artists UAS-5573, US/ 1971 Harvest SHVL-797, UK.

Source: ?
Note: As one hears the radio being tuned on this selection, a section of classical music played backwards is heard. In a radio interview ELO member Jeff Lynne could not remember which classical piece was used. The album was reissued as No answer (1972 United Artists UAS-5573, 1978 Jet JZ-35524, US). This piece also appears on the compilation album The light shines on (1977 Harvest SHSM-2015, UK).

EMERSON, LAKE & POWELL

S093 "Mars, the bringer of war." Emerson, Lake & Powell. 1986 Polydor 422-829-297-1-Y-1, US/ 1986 Polydor POLD-5191, UK.

Source: Holst/The planets, op. 32, Mars the bringer of war
Note: Drummer Cozy Powell was once a member of the rock group Rainbow and is regrouped with Greg Lake and Keith Emerson of Emerson, Lake & Palmer (ELP).

ERICKSON, RAYMOND

S094 The Erickson tapes. 1974 Syntonic Research SD-66100, US.

Contents: My Lady Carey's dompe (English anon.

1525 AD) -- Suite of Renaissance dances (Ammerbach) -- Trio sonata in E flat major (J. S. Bach) -- Sonata in C major K. 545 (Mozart)
Note: Renaissance, baroque and classical music is performed on SR synthesizer.

EUROPE

S095 "The flight of the bumblebee." 199? live album release pending.

Source: Rimsky-Korsakov/The legend of Tsar Saltan, first theme (Flight of the bumblebee)
Note: Kee Marcello performs this speedy arrangement as part of an electric guitar solo between the songs "Carrie" and "On the loose" on the music video-cassette Europe: the final countdown world tour (1987 CBS Music Video 19V49005, US).

FAITHFULL, MARIANNE

S096 "Ballad of the soldier's wife." Lost in the stars: the music of Kurt Weill. 1985 A&M SP9-5104, US/ 1985 A&M AMA-5104, UK.

Source: Weill/The threepenny opera, Ballad of the soldier's wife
Note: Marianne Faithfull performs with Chris Spedding on this recording.

FALCO

S097 "Rock me Amadeus." Falco3. 1985 A&M SP-5105, US/ 1985 A&M AMA-5105, UK (albums); 1985 A&M 2821, US (single); 1985 A&M SP-12150, US (12"single).

Source: Mozart
Note: This song is a mixture of classical, heavy metal and hip-hop influences. The single reached #1 on both US and UK pop charts.

S098 "Vienna calling." Falco3. 1985 A&M SP-5105, US/ 1985 A&M AMA-5105, UK (albums); 1985 A&M AM-2832, US (single); 1985 A&M SP-12150. US (12" single, B-side).

Source: J. Strauss, Jr./The Blue Danube, op. 317
Note: The introduction includes quotes from the end of the Strauss waltz played on a touch-tone phone.

FELICIANO, JOSÉ

S099 "Fireworks (from Handel's 'Fireworks suite')." Fireworks. 1970 RCA Victor LSP-4370, US.

Source: Handel/Fireworks music

FERRANTE AND TEICHER

S100 "Clair disco lune." Star wars. 1978 United Artists UA-LA855-H, US.

Source: Debussy/Suite bergamasque, Clair de lune, first theme

S101 "Moonshine sonata." Star wars. 1978 United Artists UA-LA855-H, US.

Source: Beethoven/Sonata no. 14 in C sharp minor, op. 27, no. 2 (Moonlight sonata)

FEVER TREE

S102 "Imitation situation 1 (Toccata and fugue)." Fever Tree. 1968 Uni 73024, 19?? MCA 551, US/ 1968 Uni UNLS-102, UK.

Source: J. S. Bach/Toccata and fugue in D minor, BWV 538
Note: Only a phrase from the Bach piece is used in the introduction to this song.

S103 "Where do you go?" Fever Tree. 1968 Uni 73024, 19?? MCA 551, US/ 1968 Uni UNLS-102, UK.

Source: Ravel/Bolero
Note: A short phrase from Ravel is used in this song.

FLAIRCK

S104 "Presto." Bal masqué. 1984 EMI 068-127180-1, Netherlands.

Source: Vivaldi/The four seasons, op. 8

FLEETWOOD MAC

S105 "You and I, part II." Tango in the night. 1987 Warner Bros. 25471-1, US/ 1987 Warner Bros. WX-65, UK.

Source: Tchaikovsky/Nutcracker suite, op. 71a, March of the wooden soldiers
Note: An underlying rhythmic theme in this song is reminiscent of the classical theme.

FOCUS

S106 "Father Bach." Mother Focus. 1975 Atco SD36-117, US/ 1975 Polydor 2302-036, UK.

Source: J. S. Bach

FRANKLIN, ARETHA

S107 "Ave Maria." One Lord, one faith, one baptism. 1987 Arista AL-8497, US/ 1987 Arista 208715, UK.

Source: Schubert/Ave Maria (op. 52, no. 6)

GARFUNKEL, ART

S108 "Feuilles-oh/Do space men pass dead souls on their way to the moon?" Angel Clare. 1973 Columbia PC(KC)-31474, US/ 1973 CBS 69021, UK.

Source: J. S. Bach
Note: A variation of a Bach melody forms a break in the middle of this song.

GAZEBO

S109 "I like Chopin." Gazebo. 1983 Baby BABLP-4000 (album); 1983 Baby 4 (7" single), 1983 Baby 412 (12" single disco mix), UK.

Source: Chopin ?
Note: Piano interludes in this song have a Chopin-like quality.

GLEESON, PATRICK

S110 Vivaldi's the four seasons. 1982 Varèse Sarabande VCDM-1000.100, US.

Source: Vivaldi/The four seasons, op. 8, no. 1-4
Note: This album is a synthesizer arrangement of Vivaldi's work.

GOLDSTEIN, WILLIAM

S111 "Brandenburg concerto no. 3 - allegro." Switched on classics. 1987 Pro-Arte CDD-338, US (CD).

Source: J. S. Bach/Brandenburg concerto no. 3 in G major, BWV 1048, Allegro

S112 "Brandenburg concerto no. 5: Mvt. I-III." Switched on classics. 1987 Pro-Arte CDD-338, US (CD).

Source: J. S. Bach/Brandenburg concerto no. 5 in D major, BWV 1050

S113 "Fantasia on Brahms lullaby." Switched on classics. 1987 Pro-Arte CDD-338, US (CD).

Source: Brahms/Lullaby (Cradle song)

S114 "March to the scaffold." Switched on classics. 1987 Pro-Arte CDD-338, US (CD).

Source: Berlioz/Symphonie fantastique, op. 14, mvt. 4, first theme (March to the scaffold)

S115 "Rhapsody on a theme of Paganini (var. 18)." Switched on classics. 1987 Pro-Arte CDD-338, US (CD).

Source: Rachmaninoff/Rhapsody on a theme of Paganini (var. 18), op. 43

S116 "Toccata and fugue in D minor." Switched on classics. 1987 Pro-Arte CDD-338, US (CD).

Source: J. S. Bach/Toccata and fugue in D minor, BWV 538

S117 "Variations on a theme." Switched on classics. 1987 Pro-Arte CDD-338, US (CD).

Source: Purcell/Variations on a theme

S118 "William Tell overture." Switched on classics. 1987 Pro-Arte CDD-338, US (CD).

Source: Rossini/William Tell overture

HAGEN, NINA

S118A "Ave Maria." Nina Hagen. 1989 Mercury 838-505-1, UK and Germany.

Source: Schubert/Ave Maria (op. 52, no. 6)

S118B "Inserts from: Aram Khachaturian, Gayne - Sabre dance." Nina Hagen in ekstasy. 1985 Columbia BFC-40004, US/ 1985 CBS 26421, UK/ 1985 CBS 26468, Germany.

Source: Khatchaturian/Gayne ballet, Sabre dance
Note: These inserts appear on the album between the pieces "The Lord's prayer" and "Gott im Himmel."

HAKE, ARDELL

S119 "Nutcracker." Switched on Christmas. 1988 Pro-Arte CDD-428, US (CD).

Source: Tchaikovsky/Nutcracker suite, op.71a
Note: This piece is a synthesizer interpretation.

HAMARI, JULIA

S120 Mozartrock. 1986 Denon CO-1333, US (CD).

Source: Mozart/selections from The magic flute, Don Giovanni, The marriage of Figaro, The abduction from the Seraglio, and Così fan tutte; Flies/Wiegenlied (erroneously attributed to Mozart)
Contents: Die Zauberflöte: Der Hölle Rache -- Don Giovanni: Vedrai, carino -- Don Giovanni: Là ci darem la mano -- Le nozze di Figaro: Deh, vieni, non tardar -- Le nozze di Figaro: Voi, che sapete -- Le nozze di Figaro: Non so più -- Die Entführung aus dem Serail: Welche Wonne welche Lust -- Die Zauberflöte: Bei Männern, welche Liebe fühlen -- Così fan tutte: Una donna -- Così fan tutte: E amore un landroncello -- Wiegenlied
Note: These arias in contemporary pop arrangements are performed by opera singer Julia Hamari with the Péter Sipos Group.

HARPERS BIZARRE

S121 "Peter and the wolf." Feelin' groovy. 1967 Warner Bros. W-1693 (mono), WS-1693 (stereo), US.

Source: Prokofiev/Peter and the wolf, op. 67, first theme (Peter)

IMPOSSIBLES

S122 "The Hallelouie chorus." Best of Louie, Louie. 1983 Rhino RNEP-605, US.

Source: Handel/Messiah, Hallelujah chorus

JOPLIN, JANIS

S123 "Summertime." Cheap thrills. 1968 Columbia PC(KCS)-9700, US/ 1968 CBS 63392, UK.

Source: Gershwin/Porgy and Bess, Summertime
Note: Joplin's first recording was performed with Big Brother and the Holding Company. This song also appears on Joplin in concert (1972 Columbia C2X-31160, US/ 1972 CBS 67241, UK), Janis Joplin's greatest hits (1973 Columbia PC(KC)-32168, US/ 1973 CBS 65470, UK) and on the videocassette Janis--the way she was (1987 MCA Home Video 80080, US) which was originally released as a film in 1974.

KAISER, HENRY, BAND

S124 "Nr. 2 klavierstuck III." Heart's desire. 1990 Reckless RECK-19, US and UK.

Source: Stockhausen/Nr. 2 klavierstück III

KAJEM

S125 Church organ + synthesizer + rhythm. 1987 Racket RRK-15.032, Germany.

Source: J. S. Bach; C. P. E. Bach; Beethoven; Fauré; Widor; Mozart; Lemmens; Rheinberger; Handel; Boëllmann

KIMERA & THE OPERAIDERS

S126 "Ah non giunge." Hits on opera. 1985 Stylus SMR-8505, UK.

Source: Bellini/La sonnambula, Ah! non giunge
Note: All pieces on this album were recorded with the London Symphony Orchestra.

S127 "Air des clochettes." Hits on opera. 1985 Stylus SMR-8505, UK.

Source: Delibes/Lakmé, act 2

S128 "L'amour est un oiseau (Habañera)." Hits on opera. 1985 Stylus SMR-8505, UK.

Source: Bizet/Carmen, L'oiseau rebelle (Habañera)

S129 "Ave Maria." Hits on opera. 1985 Stylus SMR-8505, UK.

Source: Gounod (J. S. Bach)/Ave Maria

S130 "Ave Maria." Hits on opera. 1985 Stylus SMR-8505, UK.

Source: Schubert/Ave Maria (op. 52, no. 6)

S131 "Caro nome" and "Reprise-Caro nome." Hits on opera. 1985 Stylus SMR-8505, UK.

Source: Verdi/Rigoletto, Caro nome

S132 "Chanson bohème." Hits on opera. 1985 Stylus SMR-8505, UK.

Source: Bizet/Carmen, Chanson bohème

S133 "Couplets-Escamillo's song." Hits on opera. 1985 Stylus SMR-8505, UK.

Source: Bizet/Carmen, Escamilio's song

S134 "La donna è mobile." Hits on opera. 1985 Stylus SMR-8505, UK.

Source: Verdi/Rigoletto, La donna è mobile

S135 "Excerpt-Vestia la giubba." Hits on opera. 1985 Stylus SMR-8505, UK.

Source: Leoncavallo/I Pagliacci, Vesti la giubba

S136 "The flower duet." Hits on opera. 1985 Stylus SMR-8505, UK.

Source: Delibes/Lakmé

S137 "Hölle Rache." Hits on opera. 1985 Stylus SMR-8505, UK.

Source: Mozart/The magic flute, Der Hölle Rache

S138 "The humming chorus." Hits on opera. 1985 Stylus SMR-8505, UK.

Source: Puccini/Madame Butterfly, The humming chorus

S139 "J'ai perdu mon Eurydice." Hits on opera. 1985 Stylus SMR-8505, UK.

Source: Gluck/Orfeo ed Euridice (Orpheus), act 1

S140 "Largo et factotum." Hits on opera. 1985 Stylus SMR-8505, UK.

Source: Rossini/Barber of Seville, Largo et factotum

S141 The lost o?era (The lost opera). 1985 MCA (TLO Productions) 23584, US (12" single).

Note: This recording with the London Symphony Orchestra features disco music arrangements of popular opera excerpts. Franck Pourcel conducts. Shorter versions of the "Club Raider mix/European mix" are also available as a 7" single. "Operature 1", "Operature 2", "Operature 3" and "Operature 4" also appear on Hits on opera (1985 Stylus SMR-8505, UK).

S142 "Nun's chorus." Hits on opera. 1985 Stylus SMR-8505, UK.

Source: J. Strauss, Jr./Casanova

S143 "Overture-Madame Butterfly." Hits on opera. 1985 Stylus SMR-8505, UK.

Source: Puccini/Madame Butterfly

S144 "Prelude no. 1." <u>Hits on opera</u>. 1985 Stylus SMR-8505, UK.

Source: J. S. Bach/Prelude no. 1

S145 "Sempre libera." <u>Hits on opera</u>. 1985 Stylus SMR-8505, UK.

Source: Verdi/La Traviata, Sempre libera

S146 "Un bel di." <u>Hits on opera</u>. 1985 Stylus SMR-8505, UK.

Source: Puccini/Madame Butterfly, Un bel di

S147 "Va pensiero." <u>Hits on opera</u>. 1985 Stylus SMR-8505, UK.

Source: Verdi/Nabucco, Va pensiero

KING CRIMSON

S148 "The devil's triangle." <u>In the wake of Poseidon</u>. 1970 Atlantic SD-8266, US/ 1970 Island ILPS-9127, UK.

Source: Holst/The planets, op.32, Mars the bringer of war
Note: A reissue of this album is available (198? Editions EG EGKC-2, US/ 198? Editions EG 2302-058, UK).

KRAUSE, DAGMAR

S149 "Surabaya Johnny." <u>Lost in the stars: the music of Kurt Weill</u>. 1985 A&M SP9-5104, US/ 1985 A&M AMA-5104, UK.

Source: Weill/Happy end, Surabaya Johnny

LATIN RASCALS

S150 "Arabian knights." <u>Bach to the future!</u> 1987 Tin Pan Apple 831-571-1 (album); 1987 Tin Pan Apple 885981-7 (7" single), 885981-1, 889661-1 (12 " singles), US.

Source: Tchaikovsky/Marche slave, op. 31

S151 "Bach to the future." <u>Bach to the future!</u> 1987 Tin Pan Apple 831-571-1, US.

Source: J. S. Bach/Toccata and fugue in D minor, BWV 538

S152 "Classical con fusion." Bach to the future! 1987 Tin Pan Apple 831-571-1, US.

Source: Rossini/William Tell overture; Bizet/Carmen, Toreador song; Khatchaturian/Gayne ballet, Sabre dance; Tchaikovsky/1812 overture, op. 49

S153 "Death of a rascal." Bach to the future! 1987 Tin Pan Apple 831-571-1, US.

Source: Gounod/Funeral march of a marionette

S154 "Joy O. D." Bach to the future! 1987 Tin Pan Apple 831-571-1, US.

Source: Beethoven/Symphony no. 9 in D minor, op. 125, mvt. 4, first theme (Ode to joy)

S155 "A little night noise." Bach to the future! 1987 Tin Pan Apple 831-571-1, US.

Source: Mozart/Serenade no. 13 in G major, K. 525 (Eine kleine nachtmusik)

S156 "Macho Mozart." Bach to the future! 1987 Tin Pan Apple 831-571-1 (album); 885567-7 (7" single), 885567-1 (12" single), US.

Source: Mozart/Piano sonata no. 11 in A major, K. 300i (331), mvt. 3 (Rondo alla turca)

S157 "Paco bell cannon." Bach to the future! 1987 Tin Pan Apple 831-571-1, US.

Source: Pachelbel/Canon in D major

S158 "Yo Elise!" Bach to the future! 1987 Tin Pan Apple 831-571-1, US.

Source: Beethoven/Für Elise

LIGHT, CHRISTOPHER

S159 The ultimate music box. 1988 Musical Heritage Society MHS-G12264, US.

Source: as listed below
Contents: Tunes for Clay's musical clock, set 1: no. 1, 8, 5, 2 (Handel) -- Sonata for cylinder organ (Cherubini) -- Pieces for the Urban organ, H.XIX. Allegro moderato, no. 22; Presto, no. 18; Song: Warning to a girl, no. 19; Allegro, no. 24 (Haydn) -- Wellington's victory at Vittoria for panharmonicon, op. 91 (Beethoven) -- Pieces for mechanical instruments, Wq. 193. Allegro for cylinder organ, no. 29; Minuet for clockwork flute and harp,

no. 19-20; Adagio for mechanical clarinet, no. 26; Presto for clockwork harp, no. 7 (C. P. E. Bach) -- Pieces for clockwork instruments, set 1, WoO 33. Allegro, no. 3; Scherzo, no. 2; Adagio assai, no. 1 (Beethoven)
Note: Utilizing synthesizers and a sequencer, this album recreates pieces for mechanical instruments which were originally written by classical composers. Christopher Light and David Kraehenbuehl are the performers/programmers.

LIGHT, ENOCH

S160 "A little fugue for you and me." Spaced out/The music of Bach, Bacharach & the Beatles. 1969 Project 3 PR-5043SD, US.

Source: J. S. Bach/Fugue in G minor, BWV 578
Note: Light's album integrates the Moog synthesizer, the guitar, electric harpsichords, flugelhorns, etc.

S161 "Lover's concerto." Spaced out/The music of Bach, Bacharach & the Beatles. 1969 Project 3 PR-5043SD, US.

Source: J. S. Bach/Notebook for Anna Magdalena Bach, Minuet in G

S162 "My silent song." Spaced out/The music of Bach, Bacharach & the Beatles. 1969 Project 3 PR-5043SD, US.

Source: J. S. Bach/Suite no. 3 in D major for orchestra, BWV 1068, Air for the G string

S163 "Petite Paulette." Spaced out/The music of Bach, Bacharach & the Beatles. 1969 Project 3 PR-5043SD, US.

Source: J. S. Bach/Lute suite no. 1 in E minor, BWV 996, Bourrée

LONDON PHILHARMONIC ORCHESTRA

S164 "Bach to funk." A classic case of funk. 1982 Warwick WW-5130, UK.

Source: J. S. Bach/Concerto for 2 violins and orchestra

S165 "A case of romantic funk." A classic case of funk. 1982 Warwick WW-5130, UK.

Source: Tchaikovsky/Romeo and Juliet; Grieg/Morning (from Peer Gynt); Tchaikovsky/Symphony no. 5, slow movement; Tchaikovsky/Piano concerto; Borodin/ Polovetsian dances (Stranger in paradise)

S166 "A classic case of funk (Good Grieg!)." A classic case of funk. 1982 Warwick WW-5130, UK.

Source: Grieg/Piano concerto in A minor, op. 16, mvt. 1

S167 "Do that waltz thing." A classic case of funk. 1982 Warwick WW-5130, UK.

Source: Rosas/Over the waves; J. Strauss, Jr./Die Fledermaus waltz; Delibes/Coppelia; Tchaikovsky/Waltz thou the Sleeping Beauty; J. Strauss, Jr./Blue Danube; Tchaikovsky/Dance of the flowers

S168 "Fiddlin' funk." A classic case of funk. 1982 Warwick WW-5130, UK.

Source: Monti/Czardas; Brahms/Hungarian dance; Rossini/William Tell; Mozart/Rondo a la turk; Rimsky-Korsakov/Flight of the bumble bee

S169 "Funk the ninth." A classic case of funk. 1982 Warwick WW-5130, UK.

Source: Beethoven/Symphony no. 9 in D minor, op.125, mvt. 4

S170 "Funky Brandenburg." A classic case of funk. 1982 Warwick WW-5130, UK.

Source: J. S. Bach/Brandenburg concerto no. 3 in G major, BWV 1048

S171 "Funky guide to the orchestra." A classic case of funk. 1982 Warwick WW-5130, UK.

Source: Purcell

S172 "The funky swan." A classic case of funk. 1982 Warwick WW-5130, UK.

Source: Tchaikovsky/Swan lake; Grieg/Hall of the mountain king (from Peer Gynt); Mozart/Eine kleine nachtmusik, mvt. 4; Tchaikovsky/1812 finale; Beethoven/Symphony no. 5, mvt. 1; Mozart/Symphony no. 40, mvt. 1

S173 "The Gilbert and Sullivan case." A classic case of funk. 1982 Warwick WW-5130, UK.

Source: Gilbert and Sullivan/A modern major general;

A wandering minstrel I; Three little maids; Flowers that blossom; A policeman's lot is not a happy one; Tit willow

S174 "One fine day." _A classic case of funk_. 1982 Warwick WW-5130, UK.

Source: Puccini/Madame Butterfly, Un bel di

S175 "A patriotic case of funk 1st movement." _A classic case of funk_. 1982 Warwick WW-5130, UK.

Source: Parry/Jerusalem; Arne/Rule Britannia; Elgar/Pomp and circumstance (Land of hope and glory)

S176 "Radetzky's got a brand new bag." _A classic case of funk_. 1982 Warwick WW-5130, UK.

Source: J. Strauss, Sr./Radetzky march

LORD, JON

S177 "Continuo on B.A.C.H." _Windows_. 1974 EMI Electrola IC-062-95-634, Germany/ 1974 Purple TPSA-7513, UK.

Source: J. S. Bach/The art of the fugue, BWV 1080, no. 19

LYNNE, JEFF

S178 "September song." _Armchair theatre_. 1990 Reprise 9-26184-1, US/ 1990 Reprise WX-347, UK.

Source: Weill/Knickerbocker holiday, September song
Note: George Harrison accompanies Jeff Lynne on slide guitar.

MAFFIA

S179 "Hallelujah." _Pay it all back, vol. 1_. 1984 On-U Sound LP-37, UK.

Source: Handel/Messiah, Hallelujah chorus

S180 "Jerusalem." _Learning to cope with cowardice_. 1983 On-U Sound LP-24, UK (with Mark Stewart).

Source: Parry/Jerusalem
Note: This piece also appears on the compilations _Pay it all back, vol. 1_ (1984 On-U Sound LP-37, UK) and _Mark Stewart + Maffia_ (1986 Upside UP-60005-1, US).

S181 "Stranger." S.A.N.D. 1987 Upside UP-60013-1, US (with Mark Stewart).

Source: Satie/Gymnopédie no. 1 (sometimes known as no. 3)

MALMSTEEN, YNGWIE J., ('S RISING FORCE)

S182 "Dreaming (Tell me)." Odyssey. 1988 Polydor 835-451-1, US/ 1988 Polydor POLD-5224, UK.

Source: J. S. Bach/Fugue in G minor, BWV 578; Beethoven/Für Elise
Note: The introduction features the Bach quote in bars 1-5 and the Beethoven quote in bar 12. A later section is reminiscent of Villa-Lobos' guitar "Prelude no. 3." A live version appears on Trial by fire: live in Leningrad (1989 Polydor 839726-1, US and UK).

S183 "Far beyond the sun." Rising Force. 1984 Polydor 825-324-1-Y1, US/ 1984 IMS/Verve 825-324-1, UK.

Source: J. S. Bach/Toccata and fugue in D minor, BWV 538
Note: Only a short phrase from the Bach piece is heard in this heavy metal instrumental. A live version appears on Trial by fire: live in Leningrad (1989 Polydor 839726-1, US and UK).

S184 "Icarus' dream suite opus 4." Rising Force. 1984 Polydor 825-324-1-Y1, US/ 1984 IMS/Verve 825-324-1, UK.

Source: Albinoni/Adagio in G minor for strings and organ
Note: Malmsteen, a Swedish guitar virtuoso, draws from both classical and heavy metal influences in this instrumental.

MANDOZZI, GRAZIANO

S185 Bach/Handel 300. 1985 Deutsche Grammophon 415-110-1, Germany.

Source: J. S. Bach and Handel/ as listed below
Contents: Allegro, mvt. 1 from Brandenburg concerto no. 2 in F major (J. S. Bach) -- Prelude in C minor from 6 kleine Präludien BWV 934 (J. S. Bach) -- Chorale "Jesu joy of man's desiring" from Cantata BWV 147 (J. S. Bach) -- Country dance I/II in G minor/major (Handel) -- Menuet in F major (Handel) -- Bourrée in F major from The water music (Handel) -- Vivace, mvt. 1 from the Concerto for 2 violins in D minor (J. S. Bach) -- Allegro, mvt. 4 from the Flute sonata in F major op. 1 no. 11 (Handel) --

Aria: Bist du bei mir (J. S. Bach attrib.) -- Badinerie from the Suite for orchestra no. 2 in B minor (J. S. Bach) -- Hallelujah chorus from Messiah (Handel) -- Andante, mvt. 1 from Sonata a 5 (violin concerto) in B flat major (Handel) -- Sinfonia "The arrival of the Queen of Sheba" from Solomon (Handel) -- Minuet in G major from the Notenbüchlein der Anna Magdalena Bach (J. S. Bach) -- Aria, mvt. 1: Jauchzet Gott in allen Landen from Cantata BWV 51 (J. S. Bach) -- Adagio, mvt. 3 from the Sonata for viola da gamba and harpsichord in C major (Handel) -- Andante allegro, mvt. 1 from the Organ (harp/synthesizer) concerto in B flat major, op. 4, no. 6 (Handel) -- Air and variations from The harmonious blacksmith (Handel)
Note: This album of synthesizer music recorded to celebrate the 300th birthdays of Bach and Handel adds a contemporary sound to the classics.

MARILLION

S186 "Intro-La gazza ladra." The thieving magpie. 1988 Capitol C12L-91463, US/ 1988 EMI MARL-1, UK.

Source: Rossini/La gazza ladra (The thieving magpie)

MARSTON, STEPHEN

S187 "Hallelujah chorus." Switched on Christmas. 1988 Pro-Arte CDD-428, US (CD).

Source: Handel/Messiah, Hallelujah chorus
Note: This piece is a synthesizer interpretation.

McLAREN, MALCOLM

S188 "Algernon's simply awfully good at algebra." Waltz darling. 1989 Epic OE-45247, US/ 1989 Epic EPC-1460736, UK.

Source: J. Strauss, Jr./Blue Danube waltz, op. 317, no. 1, second theme

S189 "Boys' chorus." Fans. 1984 Island 90242-1, US/ 1984 Charisma MMDL-2, UK.

Source: Puccini/Turandot, La sui monti dell' est

S190 "Call a wave." Waltz darling. 1989 Epic OE-45247, US/ 1989 Epic EPC-1460736, UK.

Source: Lehár/Merry widow waltz

S191 "Carmen." Fans. 1984 Island 90242-1, US/ 1984 Charisma MMDL-2, UK.

Source: Bizet/Carmen, L'oiseau rebelle (Habañera)

S192 "Death of Butterfly." <u>Fans</u>. 1984 Island 90242-1, US/ 1984 Charisma MMDL-2, UK.

Source: Puccini/Madame Butterfly, Tu tu piccolo

S193 "Fans." <u>Fans</u>. 1984 Island 90242-1, US/ 1984 Charisma MMDL-2, UK.

Source: Puccini/Turandot, Nessun dorma

S194 "House of the Blue Danube." <u>Waltz darling</u>. 1989 Epic OE-45247, US/ 1989 Epic EPC-1460736, UK.

Source: J. Strauss, Jr./Blue Danube waltz, op. 317, no. 1, first theme; no. 2, second theme; no. 5, second theme; introduction
Note: On this instrumental Malcolm McLaren is joined by the "Bootzilla Orchestra" featuring Bootsy Collins and Jeff Beck.

S195 "Lauretta." <u>Fans</u>. 1984 Island 90242-1, US/ 1984 Charisma MMDL-2, UK (albums); 1984 Island 096915, US/ 1984 Virgin/Charisma MALC-512, UK (12" singles).

Source: Puccini/Gianni Schicchi, O mio babbino caro

S196 "Madam Butterfly." <u>Fans</u>. 1984 Island 90242-1, US/ 1984 Charisma MMDL-2, UK (albums); 1984 Island 096915, US/ 1984 Virgin/Charisma MALC-512, UK (12" singles).

Source: Puccini/Madame Butterfly, Un bel di vedremo
Note: This song integrates lyrics relating to Puccini's opera story, the actual aria sung by an opera singer, and rock devices know as rapping and hip-hop (break dance) rhythms. A 12" picture disc of the single (1984 Virgin/Charisma MALCS5, UK) was released.

S197 "Shall we dance." <u>Waltz darling</u>. 1989 Epic OE-45247, US/ 1989 Epic EPC-1460736, UK.

Source: J. Strauss, Jr./Emperor waltzes, op. 437, no. 1, first and second themes

MOORE, VINNIE

S198 "April sky." <u>Time odyssey</u>. 1988 Squawk/Polygram 834-634-1, US/ 1988 Squawk/Vertigo/Phonogram VERH-60, UK.

Source: J. S. Bach/Suite no. 3 in D major for

orchestra, BWV 1068, Air for the G string; Piano concerto no. 5 in F minor, BWV 1056, mvt. 2

MORODER, GIORGIO

S199 "The duel." Electric dreams (film soundtrack). 1984 Virgin/Epic SE-39600, US/ 1984 Virgin V-2318, UK.

Source: J. S. Bach/Notebook for Anna Magdalena Bach, Minuet in G
Note: This instrumental is a duet written for cello and computer/synthesizer. A videocassette of the film Electric dreams (1985 MGM/UA Home Video AKAG-404, US) was released.

MOVE

S200 "Cherry Blossom Clinic revisited." Shazam. 1970 A&M SP-4259, US/ 1970 Regal Zonophone SLRZ-1012, UK.

Source: J. S. Bach/Jesu joy of man's desiring (from cantata no. 147); Tchaikovsky/Nutcracker suite, op. 71a
Note: Only snatches of the two classical pieces are quoted. The album was reissued (197? Polydor 2310-012) and is part of the two-record set Move/Shazam (1972 Cube TOOFA-5/6, UK).

MURPHY, WALTER

S201 "Classical dancin'." Walter Murphy's discosymphony. 1979 N.Y. International BXL1-3506, US.

Source: Brahms/Symphony no. 3 in F, op. 90

MUTANT ROCKERS

S202 "Classical scratch (first movement)." 1985 Beggars Banquet BEG-127-T, UK (12" single).

Source: Handel/Messiah, Hallelujah chorus; Beethoven/Symphony no. 5 in C minor, op. 67, mvt. 1, first theme; Handel/Water music, hornpipe; Elgar/Pomp and circumstance, op. 39, no. 1, 2nd theme; Dvorák/Symphony no. 9 (old no. 5) in E minor (from the New World), op. 95, mvt. 4
Note: Break-dance rhythms over "scratch-"altered themes are heard on this piece. A bust of Beethoven is pictured on the album jacket with the inscription "those classical chaps were jolly funky--all they needed was the beat."

NEW WORLD ORCHESTRA

S203 "Allegro for Joseph." Beethoven forever. c1987, 1988 Wergo Spectrum SM-1064-50, Germany (CD).

Source: Beethoven/Sonata no. 1 in F minor, op. 2, no. 1
Note: This album was arranged for synthesizer by Delle Haensch and Klaus Netzle.

S204 "Another menuetto." Beethoven forever. c1987, 1988 Wergo Spectrum SM-1064-50, Germany (CD).

Source: Beethoven/Minuet in G

S205 "Beat of joy." Beethoven forever. c1987, 1988 Wergo Spectrum SM-1064-50, Germany (CD).

Source: Beethoven/Symphony no. 9 in D minor, op. 125

S206 "Eliza comes again." Beethoven forever. c1987, 1988 Wergo Spectrum SM-1064-50, Germany (CD).

Source: Beethoven/Für Elise

S207 "The fifth." Beethoven forever. c1987, 1988 Wergo Spectrum SM-1064-50, Germany (CD).

Source: Beethoven/Symphony no. 5 in C minor, op. 67

S208 "A menuetto." Beethoven forever. c1987, 1988 Wergo Spectrum SM-1064-50, Germany (CD).

Source: Beethoven/Sonata no. 7 in D, op. 10, no. 3, mvt. 3 (minuetto)

S209 "Moonlight serenada." Beethoven forever. c1987, 1988 Wergo Spectrum SM-1064-50, Germany (CD).

Source: Beethoven/Sonata no. 14 in C# minor, op. 27, no. 2 (Moonlight sonata)

S210 "Quite pathetic." Beethoven forever. c1987, 1988 Wergo Spectrum SM-1064-50, Germany (CD).

Source: Beethoven/Sonata no. 8 in C minor, op. 13 (Pathétique)

S211 "Swingin' Beethoven." Beethoven forever. c1987, 1988 Wergo Spectrum SM-1064-50, Germany (CD).

Source: Beethoven/Allegro con brio

S212 "Vivace." Beethoven forever. c1987, 1988 Wergo Spectrum SM-1064-50, Germany (CD).

Source: Beethoven/Sonata no. 13 in E flat, op. 27, no. 1

NOMI, KLAUS

S213 "The cold song." Klaus Nomi. 1981 RCA LP-6026, UK/ 1981 RCA PL-37556, Germany.

Source: Purcell/The cold song

S214 "Death." Simple man. 1982 RCA LP-6061, UK/ 1982 RCA PL-37702, Germany.

Source: Purcell/Dido and Aeneas

S215 "From beyond." Simple man. 1982 RCA LP-6061, UK/ 1982 RCA PL-37702, Germany.

Source: Dowland/If my complaints

S216 "Return." Simple man. 1982 RCA LP-6061, UK/ 1982 RCA PL-37702, Germany.

Source: Dowland/If my complaints

S217 "Wayward sisters." Simple man. 1982 RCA LP-6061, UK/ 1982 PL-37702, Germany.

Source: Purcell/Dido and Aeneas

OLDFIELD, MIKE

S218 "North Star." Platinum. 1979 Virgin V-2141, UK.

Source: Glass/North Star
Note: Fragments of Glass' music are performed in disco style. "North Star" also appears on The complete Mike Oldfield (1985 Virgin MOC-1, US and UK).

S219 "William Tell overture." The complete Mike Oldfield. 1985 Virgin CDMOC-1, US and UK (CD).

Source: Rossini/William Tell overture
Note: This piece appears on Oldfield's compact disc only.

101 STRINGS

S220 "Back beat symphony." Back beat symphony: rock and roll in the sound of magnificence. 19?? Somerset SF-11500, US.

Source: Tchaikovsky/Symphony no. 5 in E minor, op. 64

S221 "Choppin' Chopin." Back beat symphony: rock and roll in the sound of magnificence. 19?? Somerset SF-11500, US.

Source: Chopin/Fantaisie impromptu, op.66

S222 "New World rock." Back beat symphony: rock and roll in the sound of magnificence. 19?? Somerset SF-11500, US.

Source: Dvorák/Symphony no. 9 (old no. 5) in E minor, op. 95, largo

S223 "Rigoletto rock." Back beat symphony: rock and roll in the sound of magnificence. 19?? Somerset SF-11500, US.

Source: Verdi/Rigoletto

S224 "Romeo and Juliet." Back beat symphony: rock and roll in the sound of magnificence. 19?? Somerset SF-11500, US.

Source: Tchaikovsky/Romeo and Juliet

S225 "Sherabop." Back beat symphony: rock and roll in the sound of magnificence. 19?? Somerset SF-11500, US.

Source: Rimsky-Korsakov/Scherherazade, op.35, mvt. 3

S226 "Strings at the hop." Back beat symphony: rock and roll in the sound of magnificence. 19?? Somerset SF-11500, US.

Source: Tchaikovsky/Symphony no. 6 in B minor, op. 74 (Pathétique)

S227 "Swingin' at Igors." Back beat symphony: rock and roll in the sound of magnificence. 19?? Somerset SF-11500, US.

Source: Borodin/Prince Igor

S228 "Swingin' little Martha." Back beat symphony: rock and roll in the sound of magnificence. 19?? Somerset SF-11500, US.

Source: Flowtow/Martha

S229 "Twangy serenade." Back beat symphony: rock and roll in the sound of magnificence. 19?? Somerset SF-11500, US.

Source: Schubert/Serenade

OSWALD, JOHN

S230 "Spring." _Plunderphonics_. 1988 Mystery Laboratory, Canada (EP).

Source: Stravinsky/The rite of spring
Note: Oswald transformed a standard commercial recording via splicing, speed variation, overdubbing and other multi-track techniques. This EP is available to broadcasters only.

OWENS, RANDALL

S231 _Russia electronica_. 1989 Neos , US (CD).

Source: as listed below
Contents: Nutcracker suite (Tchaikovsky) -- Polovetsian dances (Borodin) -- Slavonic dances nos. 1-4 (Dvorák) -- plus others

P.F.M. (Premiata Forneria Marconi)

S232 "Alta Loma nine till five." _P.F.M. Cook_. 1974 Manticore MA6-502S1, US/ 1974 Manticore K-53506, UK.

Source: Rossini/William Tell overture

PARKS, VAN DYKE

S233 "In no man's land." _Lost in the stars: the music of Kurt Weill_. 1985 A&M SP9-5104, US/ 1985 A&M AMA-5104, UK.

Source: Weill/Johnny Johnson, In no man's land

S234 "Johnny Johnson medley." _Lost in the stars: the music of Kurt Weill_. 1985 A&M SP9-5104, US/ 1985 A&M AMA-5104, UK.

Source: Weill/Johnny Johnson

RAUNCH HANDS

S235 "Merry widow waltz." _Payday_. 1989 Crypt CRYPT-015, US.

Source: Lehár/Merry widow waltz
Note: The rhythm and bass track subtly approximates the classical melody.

REED, LOU

S236 "September song." _Lost in the stars: the music of Kurt Weill_. 1985 A&M SP9-5104, US/ 1985 A&M AMA-5104, UK.

Source: Weill/Knickerbocker holiday, September song
Note: Reed also recorded this piece on a single (1985 A&M 2781, US).

REVERBERI (Gian Piero Reverberi)

S237 "Beethoven's 7th." Stairway to heaven. 1977 United Artists UA-LA813-H, US.

Source: Beethoven/Symphony no. 7 in A major, op. 92
Note: Italian keyboardist Reverberi blends electric instruments with the Milan Symphony Orchestra.

S238 "Reverberi & Schumann, Chopin, Liszt." 1976 Pausa 7003, US (single).

Source: Schumann; Chopin; Liszt
Note: Reverberi records contemporary instrumental stylings of the above named classical composers.

RIDGWAY, STANARD

S239 "The cannon song." Lost in the stars: the music of Kurt Weill. 1985 A&M SP9-5104, US/ 1985 A&M AMA-5104, UK.

Source: Weill/The threepenny opera, The cannon song
Note: Ridgway performs with the Fowler Brothers on this recording.

RIOS, WALDO DE LOS

S240 Conciertos. 1976 Hispavox SHV-60.598, Uraguay.

Source: Concertos on this album are: Concerto for piano and orchestra no. 3 in C minor, mvt. 3 "Rondo" (Beethoven) -- Concerto for oboe and orchestra in D minor, mvt. 2 "Adagio" (Marcello) -- Concerto for piano and orchestra no. 2 in C minor, op. 18, mvt. 1 (Rachmaninoff) -- Concerto for guitar and orchestra in D major, mvt. 1 "Allegro" (Vivaldi) -- Concerto for piano and orchestra, no. 1 in E minor, op. 11, mvt. 1 "Allegro maestoso" (Chopin) -- Concerto for trumpet and orchestra in E flat major, mvt. 1 "Allegro" (Haydn) -- Concerto no. 20 for piano and orchestra in D minor, mvt. 2 "Romanza" KV 466 (Mozart) -- Brandenburg Concerto no. 2 in F major "Allegro" (J. S. Bach) -- Concerto for violin and orchestra in D major, mvts. 1 and 2 (Tchaikovsky) -- Concerto for piano and orchestra in F major, mvt. 2 (Gershwin).

S241 Sinfonias 2. 1974 Hispavox SHV-60.582, Uraguay.

Source: Symphonies on this album are: Symphony no. 1 in C minor, op. 68, mvt. 4 (adagio) andante non troppo ma con brio (Brahms) -- Symphony no. 1 in C major, op. 21, mvt. 4 (adagio allegro molto e vivace) (Beethoven) -- Symphony no. 5 in D major, op. 107 "La Reforma," mvt. 3 (adagio) (Mendelssohn) -- Symphonie Fantastique, op. 14, mvt. 3 "Un baile" (Berlioz) -- Symphony no. 7 in A major, op. 92, mvt. 2 (allegretto) (Beethoven) -- Symphony no. 6 in B minor, op. 74 Pathétique, mvt. 1 (adagio) (Tchaikovsky) -- Symphony no. 101 in D major, op. 95 ("The clock") (Haydn) -- Sinfonia Española op. 21 Andante (Lalo) -- Symphony no. 6 in F major, op. 68 "Pastoral," mvt. 5 (allegretto) (Beethoven).

RISING FORCE. See MALMSTEEN, YNGWIE J., ('S RISING FORCE)

ROCKMORE, CLARA

S242 "Berceuse." Shirleigh and Robert Moog present Clara Rockmore. 1977 Delos DEL-25437, US.

Source: Stravinsky/Firebird suite, Berceuse
Note: Rockmore performs on theremin, an early electronic instrument, and is accompanied by Nadia Reisenberg on piano. This album was reissued on CD as The art of the theremin (1987 Delos DCD-1014, US).

S243 "Berceuse." Shirleigh and Robert Moog present Clara Rockmore. 1977 Delos DEL-25437, US.

Source: Tchaikovsky/Berceuse

S244 "Chant du ménestrel." Shirleigh and Robert Moog present Clara Rockmore. 1977 Delos DEL-25437, US.

Source: Glazunov/Chant du ménestrel, op. 71

S245 "Habañera." Shirleigh and Robert Moog present Clara Rockmore. 1977 Delos DEL-25437, US.

Source: Ravel/Rapsodie espagnole, mvt. 3, first theme (Habañera)

S246 "Hebrew melody." Shirleigh and Robert Moog present Clara Rockmore. 1977 Delos DEL-25437, US.

Source: Achron/Hebrew melody, op. 33

S247 "Pantomime." Shirleigh and Robert Moog present Clara Rockmore. 1977 Delos DEL-25437, US.

Source: Falla/El amor brujo (ballet), Pantomime

S248 "Romance." Shirleigh and Robert Moog present Clara Rockmore. 1977 Delos DEL-25437, US.

Source: Wieniawski/Concerto no. 2 in D minor, op. 22, mvt. 2 (Romance)

S249 "Sérénade mélancolique." Shirleigh and Robert Moog present Clara Rockmore. 1977 Delos DEL-25437, US.

Source: Tchaikovsky/Sérénade mélancolique in B minor, op. 26

S250 "The swan." Shirleigh and Robert Moog present Clara Rockmore. 1977 Delos DEL-25437, US.

Source: Saint-Saëns/Carnaval des animaux, The swan

S251 "Valse sentimentale." Shirleigh and Robert Moog present Clara Rockmore. 1977 Delos DEL-25437, US.

Source: Tchaikovsky/Valse sentimentale, op. 51, no. 6

S252 "Vocalise/Song of Grusia." Shirleigh and Robert Moog present Clara Rockmore. 1977 Delos DEL-25437, US.

Source: Rachmaninoff/Songs, op. 34, Vocalise

ROYAL PHILHARMONIC ORCHESTRA

S253 "Aranjuez mon amour." The classics in rhythm. 1988 Arista AL9-8588, US/ 1988 Telstar STAR-2344, UK.

Source: Rodrigo/Concierto de Aranjuez

S254 "Arrival of the Queen of Sheba/Brandenburg concerto no. 3." The classics in rhythm. 1988 Arista AL9-8588, US/ 1988 Telstar STAR-2344, UK.

Source: Handel/Solomon, act III; J. S. Bach/ Brandenburg concerto no. 3 in G major, BWV 1048

S255 "Canon." The classics in rhythm. 1988 Arista AL9-8588, US/ 1988 Telstar STAR-2344, UK.

Source: Pachelbel/Canon in D major

S256 "Flight of the bumble bee." The classics in rhythm. 1988 Arista AL9-8588, US/ 1988 Telstar STAR-2344, UK.

Source: Rimsky-Korsakov/The legend of Tsar Saltan, first theme (Flight of the bumblebee)

S257 "In the hall of the mountain king." The classics in rhythm. 1988 Arista AL9-8588, US/ 1988 Telstar STAR-2344, UK.

Source: Grieg/Peer Gynt suite no. 1, op. 46, mvt. 4 (In the hall of the mountain king)

S258 "Ode to joy." The classics in rhythm. 1988 Arista AL9-8588, US/ 1988 Telstar STAR-2344, UK.

Source: Beethoven/Symphony no. 9 in D minor, op. 125, mvt. 4, first theme

S259 "Post horn galop." The classics in rhythm. 1988 Arista AL9-8588, US/ 1988 Telstar STAR-2344, UK.

Source: Koenig/Post horn galop

S260 "Sabre dance." The classics in rhythm. 1988 Arista AL9-8588, US/ 1988 Telstar STAR-2344, UK.

Source: Khatchaturian/Gayne ballet, Sabre dance

S261 "Symphony no. 5 (acid house mix)." The classics in rhythm. 1988 Arista AL9-8588, US/ 1988 Telstar STAR-2344, UK.

Source: Beethoven/Symphony no. 5 in C minor, op. 67
Note: Louis Clark conducts the Royal Philharmonic Orchestra in an Acid House arrangement of Beethoven.

S262 "Toccata and fugue in D minor." The classics in rhythm. 1988 Arista AL9-8588, US/ 1988 Telstar STAR-2344, UK.

Source: J. S. Bach/Toccata and fugue in D minor, BWV 538

S263 "William Tell overture." The classics in rhythm. 1988 Arista AL9-8588, US/ 1988 Telstar STAR-2344, UK.

Source: Rossini/William Tell overture

RUNDGREN, TODD

S264 "Call from the grave, Ballad in which Macheath begs all men for forgiveness." Lost in the stars: the music of Kurt Weill. 1985 A&M SP9-5104, US/ 1985 A&M AMA-5104, UK.

Source: Weill/The threepenny opera, Call from the grave, Ballad in which Macheath begs all men for forgiveness
Note: Todd Rundgren performs with Gary Windo on this recording.

S265 "Lord Chancellor's nightmare song." Todd. 1974 Bearsville 2BR-6952, US/ 1974 Bearsville K-85501, UK.

Source: Gilbert and Sullivan/Iolanthe, Lord Chancellor's nightmare song
Note: This album was reissued (1987 Rhino RNDA-71108, US).

SAVATAGE

S266 "Prelude to madness/Hall of the mountain king." Hall of the mountain king. 1987 Atlantic 81775-1, US/ 1987 Atlantic K-781775, UK.

Source: Holst/The planets, op. 32, first mvt. (Mars); Grieg/Peer Gynt suite no. 1, op. 46, mvt. 4 (In the hall of the mountain king)
Note: This heavy metal group draws their inspiration for the album cover and title from Grieg and borrows musical themes from Holst and Grieg for this piece of music.

SERIOUS, YAHOO

S267 "Roll and rock music." Young Einstein (film soundtrack). c1988, 1989 A&M SP-3929, US/ 1989 A&M AMA-3929, UK.

Source: Beethoven/Symphony no. 5 in C minor, op. 67, mvt. 1, first theme
Note: A videocassette of the film Young Einstein (1990 Warner Home Video 11759, US) was released.

SIGUE SIGUE SPUTNIK

S268 "Albinoni vs. Star Wars." Dress for excess. c1988, 1989 EMI E11H-48700, US/ 1988 Parlophone PCS-7328, UK.

Source: Albinoni/Adagio in G minor for strings and organ
Note: Sampling techniques were used in this song to provide a somewhat distorted Albinoni background.

SKY

S269 The Mozart album. 1987 Mercury 832-908-1, US/ 1987 Mercury MERH-116, UK.

Source: Mozart/as listed below
Contents: The marriage of Figaro: Overture -- Eine kleine nachtmusik: Rondo -- The marriage of Figaro: Non so piu, cosa son -- Symphony no. 34: Last movement -- Symphony no. 35 ("Haffner"): Andante -- The magic flute: Overture -- Eine kleine nachtmusik:

Romanza -- Horn concerto no. 4 in E-flat: Rondo -- Don Giovanni: La ci darem la mano -- A musical joke: Presto -- Come sweet May -- Alla turca: Rondo
Note: Sky appears with the Academy of St. Martin-in-the-Fields conducted by Neville Marriner.

S270 "Xango." Sky 4--forthcoming. 1982 Arista AL-9604, US/ 1982 Ariola AD-SKY4, UK.

Source: Villa-Lobos/Cançoẽs no. 4

SLY & ROBBIE

S271 "Boops (here to go)." Rhythm killers. 1987 Island 90585-1, US/ 1987 Fourth & Broadway BRLP-512, UK.

Source: Mouret/Suites de symphonies, no. 1, Rondeau (Theme from Masterpiece Theatre); Rossini/Barber of Seville overture, first theme
Note: These two themes are interjected into the song. This piece also appears on the compilation The Island story (1962-1987) (1987 Island 90684-1, US).

SPEDDING, CHRIS

S272 "Ballad of the soldier's wife." Lost in the stars: the music of Kurt Weill. 1985 A&M SP9-5104, US/ 1985 A&M AMA-5104, UK.

Source: Weill/The threepenny opera, Ballad of the soldier's wife
Note: Chris Spedding performs with Marianne Faithfull on this recording.

STEWART, MARK. See MAFFIA

STING

S273 "The ballad of Mac the Knife." Lost in the stars: the music of Kurt Weill. 1985 A&M SP9-5104, US/ 1985 A&M AMA-5104, UK.

Source: Weill/The threepenny opera, The ballad of Mac the knife
Note: Sting, of the Police, is also known as Gordon Sumner. He performs with Dominic Muldowney on this recording. In an April 1987 concert in West Germany, Sting sang with the Hamburg State Orchestra performing three songs from The threepenny opera in German and three more Weill songs in English: "The way the wind blows," "The little radio," "Lonely house."

S274 "Russians." _The dream of the blue turtles_. 1985 A&M SP-3750, US/ 1985 A&M DREAM-1, UK (albums); 1985 A&M 2799, US (A-side single); 1985 A&M 8656, US (B-side single); 1985 A&M SP-12164, US (12" single).

Source: Prokofiev/Lieutenant Kije suite, op. 60, mvt. 2, first theme, Romance

SUMMERS, ANDY

S275 "2010." _Original music from the motion picture "2010"_ (film soundtrack). 1984 A&M SP-5038, US.

Source: R. Strauss/Also sprach Zarathustra, op.30
Note: A videocassette of the film _2010_ (1985 MGM/UA Home Video MV-800591, US) was released.

SYMPHONIC ROCK ORCHESTRA

S276 "Air/Swan-Lake/Pathétique/Solvegs lied." _Symphonic Rock Orchestra in classical highlights_. 1988 PMG CD-160102, Germany (CD).

Source: J. S. Bach/Suite no. 3 in D major for orchestra, BWV 1068, Air for the G string; Tchaikovsky/Swan lake, suite from the ballet, op. 20a; Beethoven/Sonata no. 8 in C minor, op. 13 (Pathétique); Grieg/Peer Gynt suite no. 2, op. 55, mvt. 4

S277 "Etude op. 10,3/Poeme/Ave Maria." _Symphonic Rock Orchestra in classical highlights_. 1988 PMG CD-160102, Germany (CD).

Source: Chopin/Etude in E, op. 10, no. 3; Fibich/Poeme, op. 41, no. 6; Gounod (J.S. Bach)/ Ave Maria

S278 "Flight of the bumble bee/Ungarischer tanz nr. 5 Leichte Kavallerie/Carmen." _Symphonic Rock Orchestra in classical highlights_. 1988 PMG CD-160102, Germany (CD).

Source: Rimsky-Korsakov/The legend of Tsar Saltan, first theme (Flight of the bumblebee); Brahms/Hungarian dance no. 5 in F sharp minor; von Suppé/Light cavalry overture; Bizet/Carmen

S279 "Kaiser-Walzer op. 437/Jäger-Polka op. 373/Perpetuum mobile op. 257/Tritsch-Tratsch Polka op. 214/ Pizzicato Polka/Unter Donner und Blitz op. 324." _Symphonic Rock Orchestra in classical highlights_. 1988 PMG CD-160102, Germany (CD).

Source: J. Strauss, Jr./as above

S280 "The Moldau/Scheherazade/Nabucco." Symphonic Rock Orchestra in classical highlights. 1988 PMG CD-160102, Germany (CD).

Source: Smetana/Ma vlast, vitava no. 2 (The Moldau); Rimsky-Korsakov/Scheherazade, op. 35; Verdi/Nabucco

S281 "Sonata in C major KV330/Eine kleine nachtmusik (Serenade)/Sonata KV284/Türkischer marsch KV331." Symphonic Rock Orchestra in classical highlights. 1988 PMG CD-160102, Germany (CD).

Source: Mozart/Sonata in C major, K. 330; Serenade no. 13 in G major, K. 525 (Eine kleine nachtmusik); Sonata in D major, K. 284; Piano sonata no. 11 in A major, K. 300i (331), mvt. 3 (Rondo alla turca)

S282 "Swan-Lake/Capriccio Italien/Romeo and Juliet (ouvertüre)/6. symphony/Nutcracker suite (Trepak, The sugar-plum fairy, The Reded Flutes)/Romeo and Juliet (finale)." Symphonic Rock Orchestra in classical highlights. 1988 PMG CD-160102, Germany (CD).

Source: Tchaikovsky/Swan Lake, suite from the ballet, op. 20a; Capriccio Italien, op. 45; Romeo and Juliet (overture); Symphony no. 6 in B minor, op. 74 (Pathétique); Nutcracker suite, op. 71a; Romeo and Juliet (finale)

THOMPSON, LINDA

S283 "Les trois oiseaux de paradis." One clear moment. 1985 Warner Bros. 1-25164, US and UK.

Source: Ravel/Les trois oiseaux de paradis

TOMITA (Isao Tomita)

S284 "Adagio of the sky." Canon of the three stars. 1984 RCA Red Seal ARL1-5184, US/ Dawn chorus. 1984 RCA PL-85184, UK.

Source: Albinoni/Adagio in G minor for strings and organ

S285 "Also sprach Zarathustra: Opening." The mind of the universe: live at Linz 1984. 1985 RCA Red Seal ARL1-5461, US/ 1985 RCA RL-85461, UK.

Source: R. Strauss/Also sprach Zarathustra, op. 30
Note: This piece also appears on Tomita's greatest hits CD (1986 RCA Red Seal 5660-2-RC, US [CD]) as

"Also sprach Zarathustra: fanfare." A live version of "Also sprach Zarathustra: fanfare" appears on Tomita live in New York - Back to the earth (1988 RCA Victor Red Seal 7717-1-RC, US).

S286 "Canon of the three stars." Canon of the three stars. 1984 RCA Red Seal ARL1-5184, US/ Dawn chorus. 1984 RCA PL-85184, UK.

Source: Pachelbel/Canon in D major
Note: This piece also appears on Tomita's greatest hits CD (1986 RCA Red Seal 5660-2-RC, US [CD]) as "The Pachelbel canon."

S287 "Cosmic chorale." Canon of the three stars. 1984 RCA Red Seal ARL1-5184, US/ Dawn chorus. 1984 RCA PL-85184, UK.

Source: J. S. Bach/Jesu, joy of man's desiring (from cantata no. 147)

S288 "Dawn chorus." Canon of the three stars. 1984 RCA Red Seal ARL1-5184, US/ Dawn chorus. 1984 RCA PL-85184, UK.

Source: Villa-Lobos/Bachinanas Brasileiras no. 4: Preludio

S289 "Goin' home." Tomita live in New York - Back to the earth. 1988 RCA Victor Red Seal 7717-1-RC, US.

Source: Dvorák/Symphony no. 9 (old no. 5) in E minor (from the New World), op. 95, mvt. 2 (largo)

S290 "The lark ascending." The mind of the universe: live at Linz 1984. 1985 RCA Red Seal ARL1-5461, US/ 1985 RCA RL-85461, UK.

Source: Vaughan Williams/The lark ascending

S291 "Pegasus." Canon of the three stars. 1984 RCA Red Seal ARL1-5184, US/ Dawn chorus 1984 RCA PL-85184, UK.

Source: Villa-Lobos/Bachinanas Brasileriras no. 7, Toccata

S292 "La péri: fanfare." Tomita live in New York - Back to the earth. 1988 RCA Victor Red Seal 7717-1-RC, US.

Source: Dukas/La péri: fanfare

S293 "Rhapsody in blue." Tomita live in New York - Back to the earth. 1988 RCA Victor Red Seal 7717-1-RC, US.

Source: Gershwin/Rhapsody in blue

S294 The rite of spring. 199? RCA Red Seal release pending.

Source: Stravinsky/The rite of spring

S295 "The rite of spring: dance of the young girls." The mind of the universe: live at Linz 1984. 1985 RCA Red Seal ARL1-5461, US/ 1985 RCA RL-85461, UK.

Source: Stravinsky/The rite of spring, Dance of the young girls

S296 "Symphony no. 3 in D minor: fifth movement." Tomita live in New York - Back to the earth. RCA Victor Red Seal 7717-1-RC, US.

Source: Mahler/Symphony no. 3 in D minor, mvt. 5

S297 "Symphony no. 9: 'Ode to joy.'" The mind of the universe: live at Linz 1984. 1985 RCA Red Seal ARL1-5461, US/ 1985 RCA RL-85461, UK.

Source: Beethoven/Symphony no. 9 in D minor, op. 125, mvt. 4, first theme

S298 "Tristan and Isolde: Liebestod." The mind of the universe: live at Linz 1984. 1985 RCA Red Seal ARL1-5461, US/ 1985 RCA RL-85461, UK.

Source: Wagner/Tristan and Isolde, Liebestod
Note: A live version of this piece appears on Tomita live in New York - Back to the earth (1988 RCA Victor Red Seal 7717-1-RC, US).

S299 "Vela-X pulsar." Canon of the three stars. 1984 RCA Red Seal ARL1-5184, US/ Dawn chorus. 1984 RCA PL-85184, UK.

Source: Villa-Lobos/Bachinanas Brasileiras no. 4, Coral danza

S300 "Vocalise." Canon of the three stars. 1984 RCA Red Seal ARL1-5184, US/ Dawn chorus. 1984 RCA PL-85184, UK.

Source: Rachmaninoff/Songs, op. 34, Vocalise

S301 "Whistle train." Canon of the three stars. 1984 RCA Red Seal ARL1-5184, US/ Dawn chorus. 1984 RCA PL-85184, UK.

Source: Villa-Lobos/Bachinanas Brasileiras no. 2, Toccata, Little train of the Caipira

TYMES

S302 "I'm always chasing rainbows." 1962 Parkway P-7039, US (single).

Source: Chopin/Fantaisie impromptu, op. 66
Note: This single is the B-side of "Isle of love", a free bonus record with the same catalog number as the companion album Somewhere (1962 Parkway P-7039, US).

VENTURES

S303 "Also sprach Zarathustra." NASA's 25th anniversary commemorative album. 1987 Allegiance ST-72873, US.

Source: R. Strauss/Also sprach Zarathustra, op. 30

WAITS, TOM

S304 "What keeps mankind alive?" Lost in the stars: the music of Kurt Weill. 1985 A&M SP9-5104, US/ 1985 A&M AMA-5104, UK.

Source: Weill/The threepenny opera, What keeps mankind alive?

WAKEMAN, RICK

S305 Crimes of passion (film soundtrack). 1986 President RW-3, UK.

Source: Dvorák/Symphony no. 9 (old no. 5) in E minor (from the New World), op. 95
Note: This film soundtrack borrows Dvorák musical themes. The film was originally released in 1984. A videocassette of the film Crimes of passion (1985 New World Video 8418, US) was released.

WEISBERG, STEVE

S306 "Intro from Mahagonny Songspiel." Lost in the stars: the music of Kurt Weill. 1985 A&M SP9-5104, US/ 1985 A&M AMA-5104, UK.

Source: Weill/The rise and fall of the city of Mahagonny, Intro from Mahagonny Songspiel

WILBRANDT, THOMAS

S307 The electric V. 1984 Mercury 818-147-1, US and UK.

Source: Vivaldi/The four seasons, op. 8
Contents: Autumn: Leaves and lutes; Hi life!; The San Marco sequence; Phases; The celebration -- Winter: Wide white horizon; The electric harpsichord; Radio music; Dancing (at Crystal

Palace); Breaking the ice/The winter song/Beating the cold/The farewell -- Spring: The crescendo of Spring (Dawn); The electric bird/Sketches of Spring; Chant I; Chant II; Chant III; The movie; Spring water; The glass bead game; Idyll; Twilight -- Summer: The heat; 'Hot stuff'; Meditation; Thunder and lightning
Note: This new perspective on Vivaldi is composed, arranged, conducted and performed by Thomas Wilbrandt and the Philharmonia Orchestra augmented by electronic instruments.

S308 Transforming V. 1990 London 425-211-2LNL, US (CD)/ 1990 Decca 425-211-2 UK (CD).

Source: Vivaldi
Contents: Space (the meeting) -- This game (round for four alienated players) -- Balancing the night -- Silent journey -- Sequences to remember -- Music for a large room -- The minimal event -- Building -- Basic statements -- Walking, talking, standing still -- Oboes (ebony concerto) -- Close encounter -- Baroque rock (minor activities) -- Air (Mantovaldi's dream) -- Lifelines -- Landscape with chime -- Different horizons -- This atmosphere: forever -- Music for a small room -- Sea the soul -- Finally
Note: These variations on Vivaldi are arranged, conducted and performed by Thomas Wilbrandt and the Royal Philharmonic Orchestra.

WURMAN, HANS

S309 "Black key étude." The Moog strikes Bach . . . to say nothing of Chopin, Mozart, Rachmaninoff, Paganini and Prokofieff. 1969 RCA Red Seal LSC-3125, US.

Source: Chopin/Étude in G flat, op. 10, no. 5

S310 Chopin à la Moog, with lots of strings attached. 1970 RCA Red Seal LSC-3171, US.

Source: Chopin

S311 "Eine kleine nachtmusik." The Moog strikes Bach . . . to say nothing of Chopin, Mozart, Rachmaninoff, Paganini and Prokofieff. 1969 RCA Red Seal LSC-3125, US.

Source: Mozart/Serenade no. 13 in G major, K. 525 (Eine kleine nachtmusik)

S312 "Prelude." The Moog strikes Bach . . . to say nothing of Chopin, Mozart, Rachmaninoff, Paganini and Prokofieff. 1969 RCA Red Seal LSC-3125, US.

Source: Prokofiev/Prelude, op. 12, no. 7

S313 "Thirteen variations on a theme of Paganini." _The Moog strikes Bach . . . to say nothing of Chopin, Mozart, Rachmaninoff, Paganini and Prokofieff_. 1969 RCA Red Seal LSC-3125, US.

Source: Paganini/Caprice in A minor, op. 1, no. 24

S314 "Toccata and fugue in D minor." _The Moog strikes Bach. . . to say nothing of Chopin, Mozart, Rachmaninoff, Paganini and Prokofieff_. 1969 RCA Red Seal LSC-3125, US.

Source: J. S. Bach/Toccata and fugue in D minor, BWV 538

S315 "Turkish march." _The Moog strikes Bach . . . to say nothing of Chopin, Mozart, Rachmaninoff, Paganini and Prokofieff_. 1969 RCA Red Seal LSC-3125, US.

Source: Mozart/Piano sonata no. 11 in A major, K. 300i (331), mvt. 3 (Rondo alla turca)

S316 "Vocalise." _The Moog strikes Bach . . . to say nothing of Chopin, Mozart, Rachmaninoff, Paganini and Prokofieff_. 1969 RCA Red Seal LSC-3125, US.

Source: Rachmaninoff/Vocalise, op. 34, no. 14

YES

S317 "Excerpts from 'The six wives of Henry VIII.'" _Yessongs_. 1973 Atlantic SD3-100, US/ 1973 Atlantic K-60045, UK.

Source: Handel/Messiah, Hallelujah chorus
Note: A segment of the Handel piece emerges in the midst of this Rick Wakeman collage. A film of the concert is entitled _Yessongs_ (1973). A videocassette with the same title (1984 VidAmerica 7033, US) was also released.

ZAPPA, FRANK

S318 "Bolero." _The best band you never heard in your life_. 199? CD release pending.

Source: Ravel/Bolero
Note: This CD is compiled from Zappa's 1988 world tour.

S319 Broadway the hard way. 1988 Barking Pumpkin D1-74218, US/ 1989 Zappa ZAPPA-14, UK.

Source: Various classical melodies
Note: This live album intermixes classical melodies, pop tunes, TV and movie themes with Zappa's own songs.

S320 "Igor's boogie, phase one and phase two." Burnt weeny sandwich. 1969 Bizarre/Reprise RS-6370, US/ 1970 Reprise K-44083, UK.

Source: Stravinsky

S321 The music of Francesco Zappa (fl. 1763-1788). 1984 Barking Pumpkin ST-74202, US/ 1985 EMI EJ-27-0256-1, UK.

Source: Francesco Zappa/as listed below
Contents: Opus I: No. 1, mvt. 1 andante and mvt. 2 allegro con brio -- No. 2, mvt. 1 andantino and mvt. 2 minuetto grazioso -- No. 3, mvt. 1 andantino and mvt. 2 presto -- No. 4, mvt. 1 andante and mvt. 2 allegro -- No. 5, mvt. 2 minuetto grazioso -- No. 6, mvt. 1 largo and mvt. 2 minuet -- Opus IV: No. 1, mvt. 1 andantino and mvt. 2 allegro assai -- No. 2, mvt. 2 allegro assai -- No. 3, mvt. 1 andante and mvt. 2 tempo di minuetto -- No. 4, mvt. 1 minuetto
Note: The Barking Pumpkin Digital Gratification Consort conducted by Frank Zappa (actually a Synclavier) appears on this album.

ZEITGEIST

S322 "Signature one: a Mendelssohn fantasy." Duplex. 1981? Time Ghost Records Z1002, US.

Source: Mendelssohn/Songs without words, Adieu

ADDENDA (too late to be added in sequence):

GREAT KAT

S322A "Bach to the future: for geniuses only!" Beethoven on speed. 1990 RoadRacer RRD9373, US (CD).

Source: J. S. Bach ?
Note: Although this short piece sounds reminiscent of Bach, the music is credited to the Great Kat, a virtuoso thrash heavy metal guitarist.

S322B "Beethoven mosh." Beethoven on speed. 1990 RoadRacer RRD9373, US (CD).

Source: Beethoven/Symphony no. 5 in C minor, op. 67, mvt. 1

S322C "Beethoven on speed." Beethoven on speed. 1990 RoadRacer RRD9373, US (CD).

Source: Beethoven/Symphony no. 5 in C minor, op. 67, mvt. 1

S322D "Flight of the bumble-bee." Beethoven on speed. 1990 RoadRacer RRD9373, US (CD).

Source: Rimsky-Korsakov/The legend of Tsar Saltan, first theme (Flight of the bumblebee)

S322E "Funeral march." Beethoven on speed. 1990 RoadRacer RRD9373, US (CD).

Source: Chopin/Piano sonata in B flat minor, op. 35, mvt. 3

S322F "Paganini's 24th caprice." Beethoven on speed. 1990 RoadRacer RRD9373, US (CD).

Source: Paganini/Caprice in A minor, op. 1, no. 24

S322G "Sex & violins: tambourin chinois." Beethoven on speed. 1990 RoadRacer RRD9373, US (CD).

Source: Kreisler/Tambourin chinois, op. 3
Note: This instrumental is performed on 18th century violin by Katherine Thomas (The Great Kat) with piano accompaniment. Thomas studied at the Juilliard School of Music.

McLAREN, MALCOLM

S322H Malcolm McLaren presents the world famous supreme team show: Round the outside! Round the outside! 1990 Virgin 91599-2, US (CD).

Note: Early release information describes this album as a combination of rap, hip-hop, opera and excerpts from Shakespeare. McLaren used classical opera excerpts on his earlier album titled Fans (see entries on pages 31-32 of this Supplement).

II.
Classicizin' the Rock

Note: The style and quality of these versions vary widely, from strict classical style to pop style orchestral renditions. The name of the rock group or artist originally performing the song is given in parentheses after the title of the song in the album contents, except in cases where the entire album is based on one source or where the original performer of a piece is identified in the note.

BALTIMORE SYMPHONY ORCHESTRA

S323 "Twist and shout." unrecorded.

Note: Christopher Rouse's orchestral arrangement of this Isley Brothers' song is used as an encore following concert performances by the Baltimore Symphony Orchestra. No documentation of a recording could be located.

BAROQUE CHAMBER ORCHESTRA

S324 The Beatles: Seasons. 1987 Columbia SCX-6708, UK.

Contents: She loves you -- Good night -- We can work it out -- Lady Madonna -- Fool on the hill -- A hard day's night -- Michelle -- Penny Lane -- The long and winding road -- Girl -- Here comes the sun -- Hey Jude -- Carry that weight -- And I love her -- Help -- Paperback writer -- She's leaving home -- Honey pie -- Eight days a week -- Yellow submarine
Note: This album includes twenty Beatles' hits performed in the styles of Vivaldi, Handel, and Bach.

BAYLESS, JOHN

S325 Bach meets the Beatles: improvisations on Beatle melodies in the style of J. S. Bach. 1984 Pro-Arte PAD-211, US and UK.

Contents: Imagine: sinfonia -- All you need is love -- Hey Jude -- Because -- Let it be -- The long and winding road -- Penny Lane -- Yesterday -- Michelle -- Nowhere man -- And I love her -- Golden slumbers/You never give me your money -- Something -- Here, there, and everywhere -- Imagine: aria
Note: These renditions are piano improvisations.

S326 Bach on Abbey Road. 1987 Pro-Arte CDD-346, US and UK (CD).

Contents: Hard day's night -- Here comes the sun -- Good day sunshine/Daytripper -- Maxwell's silver hammer-variation 1 and 2 -- With a little help from my friends -- If I fell -- Lucy in the sky with diamonds -- She loves you/Help -- I want to hold your hand -- Can't buy me love -- I will -- Lady Madonna -- Strawberry Fields -- Eleanor Rigby -- In my life -- Good night -- A day in the life
Note: This album is composed of Beatles' melodies improvised on piano in the style of J. S. Bach. An anthology of selections from Bach meets the Beatles and Bach on Abbey Road was released as Bach, Bayless, Beatles (1989 Pro-Arte CDD-413, US and UK [CD]).

S327 Greetings from John Bayless. 1988 Megaforté/Atlantic 7-81906-2, US (CD).

Contents: The concerto: Jungleland (Allegro energico); Rosalita (Var. I Tempo di Latino, Var. II Affettuoso serenade, Var. III Allegro rapido); Sandy (Andante sostenuto); Candy's room (Toccata); Hungry heart (Un poco rubato-andante); Born to run (Andante-piu mosso allegro) -- An American portrait: The preamble ("Born in the U.S.A."); My hometown ("Amazing grace"); Westward expansion; Southern ways; A nation divided (The ascension); The final truth
Note: Bayless created these two original piano suites based on the music of Bruce Springsteen.

BERKELEY SYMPHONY ORCHESTRA

S328 Orchestral madness/Son of Serious music. 198? ICA Masterworks? JUN-1611984, US.

Note: This bootleg album features the music of Frank Zappa.

S329 Serious music. 198? ICA Masterworks OCT-31, US.

Note: This bootleg album features the music of Frank Zappa.

BERLIN PHILHARMONIC CELLISTS

S330 "Yesterday." Classics meet pops. 1986 Teldec ZK8-42957, UK (CD).

Note: This is a version of the Beatles' song.

CASTAWAY STRINGS

S331 Castaway Strings play the Elvis Presley song book. 1965? Vee Jay VJ-1113, US.

Contents: Hound dog -- Tutti frutti -- Love me tender -- Don't be cruel -- Return to sender -- It's now or never -- All shook up -- Heartbreak hotel -- Jailhouse rock -- Blue suede shoes -- Loving you

S332 Castaway Strings play the Peter, Paul, and Mary song book. 1965? Vee Jay VJ-1115, US.

Relevant contents: Lemon tree -- Blowing in the wind -- Puff the magic dragon -- If I had a hammer -- Don't think twice it's alright

DOMINGO, PLACIDO

S333 "Yesterday." Perhaps love. 1981 CBS FM-37243, US/ 1981 CBS 73592, UK.

Note: Opera tenor Plácido Domingo sings this Beatles' song with an orchestra. Perhaps love also appears as a half-speed mastered album (1981 CBS Masterworks HM-47243, US). The song also appears on the compilation A love until the end of time (1988 CBS FM-42520, US).

FAITH, PERCY, ORCHESTRA/STRINGS

S334 Angel of the morning. 1968 Columbia CS-9706, US.

Relevant contents: Angel of the morning (Merilee Rush) -- Do you know the way to San Jose (Dionne Warwick) -- MacArthur Park (Richard Harris) -- Time for livin' (Association) -- Mrs. Robinson (Simon and Garfunkel) -- Honey (Bobby Goldsboro) -- Scarborough fair/Canticle (Simon and Garfunkel)

S335 Black magic woman. 1971 Columbia CS-30800, US.

Relevant contents: Big yellow taxi (Joni Mitchell) -- Oye como va (Santana) -- Black magic woman (Santana) -- Never can say goodbye (Jackson 5)

S336 Clair. 1973 Columbia KC-32164, US.

Relevant contents: Don't let me be lonely tonight (James Taylor) -- Ben (Michael Jackson) -- Sweet surrender (Bread) -- I can see clearly now (Johnny Nash) -- 2001 (Deodato) -- Nights in white satin (Moody Blues) -- Summer breeze (Seals & Crofts) -- Super fly (Curtis Mayfield) -- Happy (Rolling Stones ?)

GOLDEN GATE STRINGS

S337 The Bob Dylan song book. 1965 Epic LN-24158 (mono), BN-26158 (stereo), US.

Contents: A hard rain's a-gonna fall -- Blowin' in the wind -- Subterranean homesick blues -- Farewell -- With God on our side -- Tomorrow is a long time -- Mr. Tambourine Man -- It's all over now, baby blue -- Don't think twice, it's all right -- It ain't me babe -- When the ship comes in -- The times they are a-changin'

S338 The Monkees song book. 1967 Epic LN-24248 (mono), BN-26248 (stereo), US.

Contents: Last train to Clarksville -- She -- This just doesn't seem to be my day -- I wanna be free -- Mary, Mary -- I'm a believer -- (I'm not your) Steppin' stone -- Saturday's child -- Auntie Grizelda -- (Theme from) The Monkees

GREENE STRING QUARTET

S339 "The Doors trilogy: Love me two times/You're lost little girl/Hello, I love you." Molly on the shore. 1988 Hannibal/Carthage HNBL-1333, US and UK.

HAMPTON STRING QUARTET

S340 What if Mozart wrote "Born to be wild"? 1988 RCA Victor Red Seal 7803-1-RC, US.

Contents: White rabbit (Jefferson Airplane) -- Stairway to heaven (Led Zeppelin) -- Stop in the name of love (Supremes) -- Honky tonk woman (Rolling Stones) -- Light my fire (Doors) -- Sunshine of your love (Cream) -- You've lost that lovin' feelin'

(Righteous Brothers) -- Born to be wild (Steppenwolf) -- Good vibrations (Beach Boys)

S341 What if Mozart wrote "Roll over Beethoven"? 1988 RCA Victor Red Seal 6675-1-RC, US.

Contents: Walk, don't run (Ventures) -- Nature boy (Bobby Darin) -- Get a job (Silhouettes) -- Roll over Beethoven (Chuck Berry) -- Stand by me (Ben E. King) -- Blue moon (Marcels) -- Earth angel (Penguins; Crew-cuts) -- The great pretender (Platters) -- To know him is to love him (Shirelles) -- Wonderful, wonderful (Johnny Mathis)
Note: This album features '50s and '60s R&B and pop songs played in the style of Beethoven, Mozart, Debussy, Pachelbel, et al.

HARNOY, OFRA

S342 The Beatles connection. 1985 Fanfare DFL-9016, Canada.

Contents: Across the universe -- Here comes the sun -- Norwegian wood/For no one -- She's leaving home -- Lucy in the sky with diamonds -- Octopus's garden -- Imagine -- Act naturally -- Hey Jude -- Golden slumbers/Carry that weight/The end
Note: Ofra Harnoy is accompanied by the Armin Electric Strings. This album was reissued as a CD with the title Electric Beatles (1988 Pro-Arte CDD-387, US).

S343 Ofra Harnoy and the Orford String Quartet play the Beatles. 1984 Fanfare DFL-6002, Canada.

Contents: Eleanor Rigby -- Here, there and everywhere -- In my life -- And I love her -- Strawberry Fields forever/The fool on the hill -- When I'm sixty-four -- Michelle -- Nowhere man -- Yesterday -- Something -- Girl
Note: Ofra Harnoy performs on violoncello accompanied by the Orford String Quartet. This album was reissued as a CD with the title Beatles by 5 (1987 Pro-Arte CDD-381, US). "Eleanor Rigby/Here, there and everywhere/When I'm sixty-four/Nowhere man" also appear on The best of Ofra Harnoy (1986 Fanfare DFL-9019, Canada). Eighteen of the pieces from the above Fanfare albums DFL-6002 and DFL-9016 were reissued as a CD with the title Beatles book (1989 Pro-Arte CDD-446, US).

HOLLYRIDGE STRINGS

S344 Oldies but goodies. 1966 Capitol T-2564 (mono), ST-2564 (stereo), US.

Contents: Blue velvet (Bobby Vinton) -- Our day will come (Ruby and the Romantics) -- Let it be me (Lettermen) -- One fine day (Chiffons) -- Sealed with a kiss (Lettermen) -- I will follow him (Little Peggy March) -- Venus (Frankie Avalon) -- Yesterday's gone (Chad and Jeremy) -- Sukiyaki (Kyu Sakamoto) -- I want to hold your hand (Beatles) -- Love letters (Elvis Presley)

KING'S SINGERS

S345 America. 1989 Angel CDC-7-49701-2, US (CD)/ 1989 EMI CDC-7497012, UK (CD).

Contents: Bridge over troubled water (Simon and Garfunkel) -- Sound of silence (Simon and Garfunkel) -- America (Simon and Garfunkel) -- Homeward bound (Simon and Garfunkel) -- If you leave me now (Chicago) -- Simon Smith and the amazing dancing bear (Tommy Boyce; Harpers Bizarre) -- Scissors cut (Art Garfunkel) -- It's lonely at the top (Randy Newman) -- Vincent (Don McLean) -- Wichita lineman (Glen Campbell)
Note: The King's Singers are accompanied by the English Chamber Orchestra and soloists.

S346 The Beatles connection. c1986, 1988 EMI Angel CDC-7-49556-2, US and UK (CD).

Contents: Penny Lane -- Mother Nature's son -- Ob-la-di, ob-la-da -- And I love her -- Help! -- Yesterday -- A hard day's night -- Girl -- Got to get you into my life -- Back in the U.S.S.R. -- Eleanor Rigby -- Blackbird -- Lady Madonna -- I'll follow the sun -- Honey pie -- Can't buy me love -- Michelle -- You've got to hide your love away -- I want to hold your hand

S347 The King's Singers believe in music. 19?? Columbia SCX-6637, UK.

Relevant contents: Short people (Randy Newman) -- All by myself (Eric Carmen) -- Lost in love (Air Supply) -- I've got the music in me (Kiki Dee) -- Goodbye yellow brick road (Elton John)

S348 "Puppet on a string." A portrait of the King's Singers. 1981 HMV Angel ESD-7103, UK.

Note: This is a version of the Elvis Presley song.

KRONOS QUARTET

S349 "Marquee moon." Rubáiyát: Elektra's 40th anniversary. 1990 Elektra 9-60940-2, US (CD)/ 1990 Elektra LP-952, UK.

Note: Kronos Quartet performs their own version of the rock group Television's "Marquee moon."

S350 "Purple haze." Kronos Quartet: Music of Sculthorpe/ Sallinen/Glass/Nancarrow/Hendrix. 1986 Nonesuch Digital 9-79111-1F, US/ 1986 Nonesuch/WEA 979-111-1, UK.

Note: Kronos Quartet performs this Jimi Hendrix composition as a string quartet. In live performances this group has also played a Frank Zappa composition, James Brown's "Sex machine" and the Rolling Stones' "Jumpin' Jack Flash."

LAST, JAMES

S351 James Last plays the greatest songs of the Beatles. 1983 Polydor POLD-5119, UK.

Contents: Eleanor Rigby -- A hard day's night -- Let it be -- Penny Lane -- She loves you -- Michelle -- Ob-la-di, ob-la-da -- Hey Jude -- Lady Madonna -- All you need is love -- Norwegian wood -- Yesterday

S352 The love album. 1972 Polydor PD-5506, US.

Relevant contents: Aquarius (Fifth Dimension) -- Mr. Tambourine Man (Bob Dylan; Byrds) -- You've lost that lovin' feeling (Righteous Brothers) -- I got you babe (Sonny and Cher)

LIGHT, ENOCH

S353 Beatles classics. 1974 Total Sound PR-5084, US.

Contents: Eleanor Rigby -- Suite: Hello goodbye/ Something/Penny Lane -- Lucy in the sky (with diamonds) -- Michelle -- Hey Jude -- Norwegian wood -- With a little help from my friends -- Let it be
Note: Arrangements are in the "classic manner."

S354 Permissive polyphonics. 1970 Project 3 PR-5048-SD, US.

Relevant contents: Marrakesh express (Crosby, Stills & Nash) -- Let it be (Beatles) -- Easy come, easy go (Cass Elliot) -- Puppet man (Fifth Dimension) -- Monday Monday (Mamas & the Papas) -- Sittin' on the dock of the bay (Otis Redding) -- Scarborough fair (Simon and Garfunkel) -- Michelle (Beatles)

LLOYD-WEBBER, JULIAN

S355 Pieces. 1985 Polydor PROLP-6, UK.

Relevant contents: Nights in white satin (Moody Blues) -- The first time ever I saw your face (Roberta Flack) -- Hello (Lionel Richie) -- Up where we belong (Joe Cocker and Jennifer Warnes) -- Bright eyes (Melissa Manchester)
Note: Julian Lloyd-Webber plays cello with the London Symphony Orchestra.

S356 "When I'm 64." Encore! Travels with my cello, volume 2. 1986 Philips 416-698-1, US and UK.

Note: Lloyd-Webber performs this Beatles' composition on cello with the Royal Philharmonic Orchestra.

LONDON PHILHARMONIC ORCHESTRA

S357 Variations. 1986 Philips 420-342-1, US and UK.

Note: Originally composed for cello and rock band, this new version of an Andrew Lloyd-Webber work is arranged for full orchestra by David Cullen. It is based on a theme of Paganini's "A minor caprice for violin."

LONDON POPS ORCHESTRA

S358 Hits philharmonic. 1985 PRT GH-663, UK.

Relevant contents: Wichita lineman (Glen Campbell) -- Eleanor Rigby (Beatles) -- Aquarius (Fifth Dimension) -- Baby, now that I've found you (Foundations) -- Something (Beatles) -- Maxwell's silver hammer (Beatles) -- Bridge over troubled water (Simon and Garfunkel) -- Let it be (Beatles) -- Long and winding road (Beatles) -- Everybody's talking (Nilsson)

LONDON SYMPHONY ORCHESTRA

S359 A classic case--the London Symphony Orchestra plays the music of Jethro Tull featuring Ian Anderson. 1985 RCA Red Seal XRL1-7067, US/ 1986 RCA RL-71134, UK.

Contents: Locomotive breath -- Thick as a brick -- Elegy/Bourrée -- Fly by night -- Aqualung -- Too old to rock 'n' roll; too young to die -- Medley: Teacher/Bungle in the jungle/Rainbow blues/Locomotive breath/Living in the past/War child
Note: The London Symphony Orchestra features Jethro Tull members Ian Anderson on flute, Martin Barre,

Peter Vitesse and Dave Pegg. The music is arranged, produced and conducted by David Palmer.

S360 Classic rock countdown. 1987 CBS MOOD-3, UK.

Contents: The final countdown (Europe) -- Take my breath away (Berlin) -- You can call me Al (Paul Simon) -- Lady in red (Chris De Burgh) -- Separate lives (Stephen Bishop) -- We don't need another hero (Tina Turner) -- It's a sin (Pet Shop Boys) -- She's not there (Zombies) -- Don't give up (Peter Gabriel) -- You're the voice (John Farnham) -- Abbey Road Medley: Golden slumbers/Carry that weight/The end (Beatles)
Note: A single was released for "You can call me Al" (1987 CBS C-ROCK-1, UK).

S361 The power of classic rock. 1985 Portrait PRT-10049, UK.

Contents: Two tribes/Relax (Frankie Goes To Hollywood) -- Drive (The Cars) -- Purple rain (Prince) -- Time after time (Cyndi Lauper) -- I want to know what love is (Foreigner) -- Born in the USA/Dancing in the dark (Bruce Springsteen) -- The power of love (Huey Lewis and the News) -- Thriller (Michael Jackson) -- Total eclipse of the heart (Bonnie Tyler) -- Hello (Lionel Richie) -- Modern girl (Sheena Easton)

S362 Rock classics. 1981 K-tel ONE-1123, UK.

Contents: Get back (Beatles) -- Layla (Derek and the Dominos) -- Stairway to heaven (Led Zeppelin) -- Baker Street (Gerry Rafferty) -- Another brick in the wall (Pink Floyd) -- Jet (Paul McCartney & Wings) -- Ruby Tuesday (Rolling Stones) -- I don't like Mondays (Boomtown Rats) -- Bright eyes (Melissa Manchester) -- Hey Jude (Beatles)
Note: This album was reissued (1987 Telescope STAR-6004, UK).

S363 Rock symphonies. 1983 K-tel ONE-1243, UK.

Contents: Born to run (Bruce Springsteen) -- For your love (Yardbirds) -- Chariots of fire (Vangelis) -- House of the rising sun (Animals) -- You really got me (Kinks) -- MacArthur Park (Richard Harris) -- Vienna (Ultravox) -- She's out of my life (Michael Jackson) -- Pictures of Lily (Who) -- Since you've been gone (Aretha Franklin) -- High heel sneakers (Jerry Lee Lewis) -- Gloria (Shadows of Knight)
Note: This album was reissued (1987 Telescope STAR-6005, UK) with "Eye of the tiger" (Survivor) substituting for "High heel sneakers."

S364 <u>We know what we like: the music of Genesis</u>. 1987 RCA 6242-1-RC, US/ 1987 RCA Red Seal RL-86242, UK.

Contents: Guide vocal -- Turn it on again -- Mad man moon -- Entangled -- Los jigos (medley): Duke's travels/Fountain of Salmacis/The knife/Unquiet slumbers/Los jigos -- Follow you, follow me -- I know what I like -- Snowbound (medley): Snowbound/Scenes from a night's dream/Say it's alright, Joe -- Horizons -- Can-Utility and the Coastliners -- Undertow -- Supper's ready
Note: The London Symphony Orchestra, conducted by David Palmer, is joined by Steve Hackett on guitar and Ian Anderson on flute. Steve Hackett was a member of an early incarnation of Genesis.

MACARTHUR, NEIL

S365 "She's not there." 1970 Deram 7524, US/ 1969 Deram DM-225, UK (singles).

Note: This orchestrated version of a Zombies' song was arranged by Neil MacArthur who is Colin Blunstone, a member of the Zombies rock group. This instrumental also appears on the compilations <u>20 one hit wonders, vol. 2</u> (1986 See for Miles CM-124, UK) and <u>Deram dayze</u> (1987 Decal/Charly LIK-9, UK).

MANCINI, HENRY, AND HIS ORCHESTRA

S366 <u>Mancini concert</u>. 1971 RCA Victor LSP-4542, US.

Relevant contents: Portrait of Simon and Garfunkel: Scarborough fair/Canticle/The sound of silence/ Mrs. Robinson/El condor pasa/Bridge over troubled water -- Medley from Jesus Christ superstar: Superstar/Everything's alright/King Herod's song/ I don't know how to love him (A. Lloyd-Webber) -- Overture from Tommy (Who)

MARBLE ARCH ORCHESTRA

S367 <u>Tomorrow's standards</u>. 1968 Liberty LST-7567, US.

Relevant contents: Hello goodbye (Beatles) -- Daydream believer (Monkees) -- Baby, now that I've found you (Foundations) -- Massachusetts (Bee Gees) -- Your mother should know (Beatles) -- Judy in disguise (with glasses) (John Fred and his Playboy Band) -- Up, up and away (Fifth Dimension) -- Whiter shade of pale (Procol Harum)

MARTIN, GEORGE, ORCHESTRA

S368 <u>Beatles to Bond and Bach</u>. 1987 Chrysalis CPCD-1604, UK (CD).

Relevant contents: Live and let die (Paul McCartney & Wings) -- Sergeant Pepper's Lonely Hearts Club Band (Beatles) -- Lucy in the sky with diamonds (Beatles) -- A day in the life (Beatles) -- Yellow submarine suite (Beatles)

MAURIAT, PAUL, AND HIS ORCHESTRA

S369 El condor pasa. 1971 Philips PHS-600-352, US.

Relevant contents: El condor pasa (Simon and Garfunkel) -- My sweet Lord (George Harrison) -- Lonely days (Bee Gees)

S370 Gone is love. 1970 Philips PHS-600-345, US.

Relevant contents: Bridge over troubled water (Simon and Garfunkel) -- Let it be (Beatles) -- Classical gas (Mason Williams)

S371 L.O.V.E. 1969 Philips PHS-600-320, US.

Relevant contents: Oh happy day (Edwin Hawkins Singers) -- Get back (Beatles) -- Aquarius (Fifth Dimension)

S372 Mauriat magic. 1968 Philips PHS-600-270, US.

Relevant contents: San Francisco (wear some flowers in your hair) (Scott McKenzie) -- Michelle (Beatles)

S373 More Mauriat. 1968 Philips PHS-600-226, US.

Relevant contents: Black is black (Los Bravos) -- Sunny (Bobby Hebb) -- Reach out I'll be there (Four Tops) -- Guantanamera (Sandpipers) -- Winchester Cathedral (New Vaudeville Band) -- Bang Bang (Cher)

S374 Prevailing airs. 1968 Philips PHS-600-280, US.

Relevant contents: Mrs. Robinson (Simon and Garfunkel) -- Honey (Bobby Goldsboro) -- Rain and tears (Aphrodite's Child) -- Eleanor Rigby (Beatles) -- Lady Madonna (Beatles)

S375 The seven seas. 1984 Philips 818-781-1, UK.

Relevant contents: So bad/Pipes of peace (Paul McCartney) -- Thriller (Michael Jackson) -- An innocent man (Billy Joel) -- Making love out of nothing at all (Air Supply) -- Say say say (Paul McCartney) -- Total eclipse of the heart (Bonnie Tyler) -- I like Chopin (Gazebo) -- Think of Laura (Christopher Cross)

S376 The soul of Paul Mauriat. 1969 Philips PHS-600-299, US.

Contents: I'm gonna make you love me (Supremes & Temptations) -- I never loved a man (Aretha Franklin) -- I've been loving you too long (Otis Redding) -- You keep me hangin' on (Supremes) -- It's a man's world (James Brown) -- When a man loves a woman (Percy Sledge) -- Respect (Otis Redding; Aretha Franklin) -- I heard it through the grapevine (Marvin Gaye; Gladys Knight and the Pips) -- In the midnight hour (Wilson Pickett) -- My girl (Temptations) -- Love child (Supremes)

S377 Windy. 1986 Philips 826-971-1, US and UK.

Relevant contents: Nikita (Elton John) -- Part-time lover (Stevie Wonder) -- Sara (Starship) -- Say you, say me (Lionel Richie)

MONTENEGRO, HUGO

S378 Dawn of Dylan. 19?? GWP ST-2003, US.

NEW PHILHARMONIA ORCHESTRA

S379 The Queen album. 1988 Siren SRNLP-22, UK.

Contents: Bohemian rhapsody -- A kind of magic -- Love of my life -- My melancholy blues -- Who wants to live forever? -- You take my breath away -- Las palabras de amor -- One year of love -- Is this the world we created? -- Radio ga ga
Note: Featured vocalist on this album is Elaine Paige.

101 STRINGS

S380 Love is blue. 1972 Alshire ST-5086, US.

Relevant contents: Love is blue (Paul Mauriat) -- A whiter shade of pale (Procol Harum).

S381 More million seller hits. 1972 Alshire S-5223, US.

Relevant contents: El condor pasa (Simon and Garfunkel) -- Bridge over troubled water (Simon and Garfunkel) -- Spinning wheel (Blood, Sweat & Tears) -- Close to you (Carpenters)

S382 More million seller hits of today. 1970 Alshire ST-5175, US.

Relevant contents: I'll never fall in love again (Dionne Warwick) -- Good morning starshine (Oliver) -- Scarborough Fayre (Simon and Garfunkel) --

Everybody's talking (Nilsson) -- Aquarius (Fifth Dimension)

S383 Plus plus plus. 1986 Alshire ALCD-18, US (CD).

Relevant contents: I'm a man (Spencer Davis Group) -- California dreamin' (Mamas & the Papas) -- San Francisco (Scott McKenzie) -- Whiter shade of pale (Procol Harum) -- Never my love (Fifth Dimension) -- Hey Jude (Beatles)

PHILHARMONIC SOUND ORCHESTRA

S384 Soft classic symphonies: the Bee Gees hits. 1989 Teldec 246-053-2, Germany (CD).

Contents: Stayin' alive -- You win again -- Medley: You should be dancing/Tragedy -- To love somebody -- How deep is your love -- Medley: Lonely days/New York mining disaster 1941/Fanny be tender with my love -- Jive talkin' -- Medley: World, I gotta get a message to you/Don't forget to remember/Words -- Nights on Broadway -- Massachusetts

POURCEL, FRANCK

S385 Aquarius. 1969 Atco SD-33-299, US.

Relevant contents: Aquarius (Fifth Dimension) -- Good morning starshine (Oliver) -- Hey Jude (Beatles)

RIDDLE, NELSON, AND HIS ORCHESTRA

S386 Contemporary sound of Nelson Riddle. 1968 United Artists UAS-6670, US.

Relevant contents: Light my fire (Doors) -- Dream a little dream of me (Cass Elliot) -- Yesterday's dreams (Four Tops) -- Halfway to paradise (Sandy Posey) -- Stoned soul picnic (Laura Nyro; Fifth Dimension) -- Sealed with a kiss (Lettermen) -- Tell someone you love them (Dino, Desi & Billy)

ROCHESTER POPS

S387 Pop go the Beatles. 1987 Pro-Arte CDD-350, US (CD).

Contents: Sgt. Pepper's Lonely Hearts Club Band/With a little help from my friends/Sgt. Pepper's Lonely Hearts Club Band reprise (Beatles) -- Michelle (Beatles) -- Eleanor Rigby (Beatles) -- Live and let die (Paul McCartney & Wings) -- And I love her (Beatles) -- When I'm 64 (Beatles) -- Got to get you into my life (Beatles) -- Yesterday (Beatles) -- Penny Lane (Beatles) -- Yellow submarine (Beatles) -- Here, there, and everywhere (Beatles) -- Please

please me/A hard day's night (Beatles)
Note: Newton Wayland conducts the Rochester Pops orchestra on this recording. The same contents, performed by the Rochester Pops Orchestra, appear on Beatles greatest hits (1989 Maxiplay CDM-8008, US [CD]) with four added pieces (Here comes the sun -- Something -- Let it be -- The long and winding road) performed by John Bayless on piano.

ROCK PHILHARMONIC

S388 Symphony on the rocks. 1987 Selected Sound 16-5016, Germany (CD).

ROYAL PHILHARMONIC ORCHESTRA

S389 Abbaphonic. 1987 Prism Entertainment CD-202, US (CD).

Contents: Abbature -- S.O.S. -- Mama mia -- Eagle -- I have a dream -- Knowing me knowing you -- Does your mother know -- Money money money -- Gimmi gimmi gimmi/Summer night city -- Chiquitita -- Finale
Note: This album is arranged and conducted by Louis Clark and features the Royal Choral Society.

S390 Classically Beatles. 1987 Prism Entertainment CD-201, US (CD).

Contents: Yesterday -- Eleanor Rigby -- Sgt. Pepper's Lonely Hearts Club Band/A little help from my friends/Lucy in the sky with diamonds -- She's leaving home -- All you need is love -- I am the walrus -- Blackbird -- The long and winding road -- Got to get you into my life/Eight days a week/Penny Lane/Yellow Submarine/Get back/Ticket to ride/Ob-la-di, ob-la-da -- Mull of Kintyre (Paul McCartney) -- She loves you/Please please me -- The fool on the hill

S391 Objects of fantasy: the music of Pink Floyd. 1989 RCA Victor 7960-2-RC, US (CD).

Contents: Run like hell -- Another brick in the wall (part 1) -- The happiest days of our lives -- Another brick in the wall (part 2) -- Goodbye blue sky -- Money -- Hey you -- Wish you were here -- On the turning away -- Shine on you crazy diamond (parts 1-5) -- When the tigers broke free -- Eclipse
Note: David Palmer conducts the Royal Philharmonic Orchestra in orchestral interpretations of the music of Pink Floyd.

S392 The R.P.O. play selected works of Rick Wakeman. 1978 A&M AMLH-68447, UK.

Contents: Orchestral suite from "The myths and legends of King Arthur and the Knights of the Round Table:" Arthur, Lady of the Lake, Merlin the magician, The last battle -- The six wives of Henry VIII: Catherine Howard, Anne Boleyn -- Orchestral suite from "Journey to the centre of the earth:" The journey, Recollection, The battle, The forest -- After the ball (from the album and film "White rock")
Note: The arranger/conductor is Richard Hartley.

ROYAL PHILHARMONIC POPS ORCHESTRA

S393 Mancini rocks the Pops. 1989 Denon CO-73078, US and UK (CD).

Contents: Walk like an Egyptian (Bangles) -- In the air tonight (Phil Collins) -- Thriller (Michael Jackson) -- Every breath you take (Police) -- Material girl (Madonna) -- With or without you (U2) -- Sweet dreams (Eurythmics) -- La Bamba (Ritchie Valens) -- On the turning away (Pink Floyd) -- It's a sin (Pet Shop Boys) -- Good old rock 'n' roll medley: Rock around the clock (Bill Haley & the Comets)/ Blue suede shoes (Elvis Presley)/Shake, rattle and roll (Bill Haley & the Comets)

S394 Pop go the Beatles. 1989 Denon CO-73324, US and UK (CD).

Contents: Beatles overture: Nowhere man/Hey Jude/And I love her/Yesterday/Eleanor Rigby/When I'm sixty-four/Honey pie/With a little help from my friends/Yellow submarine/All you need is love (Beatles) -- Can't buy me love (Beatles) -- Maxwell's silver hammer (Beatles) -- Something (Beatles) -- Got to get you into my life (Beatles) -- Imagine (John Lennon) -- Ob-la-di, ob-la-da (Beatles) -- Live and let die (Paul McCartney & Wings) -- Norwegian wood (Beatles) -- Get back (Beatles) -- I want to hold your hand (Beatles) -- Sgt. Pepper's suite (Beatles)

SOULFUL STRINGS

S395 Another exposure. 1968 Cadet LP-805 (mono), LPS-805 (stereo), US.

Relevant contents: Hello goodbye (Beatles) -- Lady Madonna (Beatles) -- Since you've been gone (Aretha Franklin) -- On the dock of the bay (Otis Redding) -- Inner light (Beatles)

Note: "Since you've been gone" is also on the compilation album The best of the Soulful Strings (197? GRT Cadet 2CA-50022, US).

S396 Groovin'. 1967 Cadet LP-796 (mono), LPS-796 (stereo), US.

Relevant contents: Groovin' (Young Rascals) -- I know I'm losing you (Temptations) -- Within you without you (Beatles)
Note: "Groovin'" and "Within you without you" are also on the compilation album The best of the Soulful Strings (197? GRT Cadet 2CA-50022, US).

S397 Paint it black. 1966 Cadet LP-776 (mono), LPS-776 (stereo), US.

Relevant contents: Paint it black (Rolling Stones) -- California dreamin' (Mamas & the Papas) -- Message to Michael (Dionne Warwick) -- Wade in the water (Ramsey Lewis) -- Love is a hurtin' thing (Lou Rawls) -- Sunny (Bobby Hebb) -- When a man loves a woman (Percy Sledge) -- Eight miles high (Byrds) -- A lover's concerto (Toys)
Note: "Paint it black," "Wade in the water" and "Eight miles high" are also on the compilation album The best of the Soulful Strings (197? GRT Cadet 2CA-50022, US).

S398 The Soulful Strings in concert. 1969 Cadet LPS-820, US.

Relevant contents: Listen here (Eddie Harris) -- I wish it would rain (Gladys Knight & the Pips; Temptations) -- You're all I need (Temptations) -- There was a time (James Brown) -- I'm a girl watcher (O'Kaysions) -- MacArthur Park (Richard Harris)
Note: "Listen here," "I wish it would rain" and "MacArthur Park" are also on the compilation album The best of the Soulful Strings (197? GRT Cadet 2CA-50022, US).

S399 The Soulful Strings play Gamble & Huff. 1970 Cadet CA-846, US.

Relevant contents: Together (Intruders) -- Turn back the hands of time (Tyrone Davis) -- One night affair (O'Jays) -- Beside you (Jerry Butler) -- Deeper in love with you (O'Jays) -- Silly silly fool (Dusty Springfield) -- Never gonna give you up (Jerry Butler) -- Hey Western Union man (Jerry Butler)
Note: Kenny Gamble and Leon Huff are the songwriters/producers for the groups listed above. "Never gonna give you up" and "Hey Western Union man" are also on the compilation album The best of the Soulful Strings (197? GRT Cadet 2CA-50022, US).

S400 String fever. 1969 Cadet LPS-834, US.

Relevant contents: Sometimes I feel like a motherless child (Richie Havens)
Note: "Sometimes I feel like a motherless child" is also on the compilation album The best of the Soulful Strings (197? GRT 2CA-5022, US).

VIENNA SYMPHONY ORCHESTRA

S401 Symphonic rock II. 1988 Stylus SMR-851, UK.

Contents: Medley: Bohemian rhapsody/We are the champions/Radio ga ga (Queen) -- Dreamer (Supertramp) -- Hard to say I'm sorry (Chicago) -- Satisfaction (Rolling Stones) -- All you need is love (Beatles) -- Stairway to heaven (Led Zeppelin) -- Space oddity (David Bowie)
Note: This album is known as Symphonic rock in Germany (1987 Dino 1441, Germany).

S402 Die Wiener Symphoniker spielen aktuelle Meisterwerke der Popmusik. 1986 Dino LP-1211, Germany.

Contents: Rock me Amadeus (Falco) -- Kyrie (Mr. Mister) -- Brothers in arms (Dire Straits) -- St. Elmo's Fire (David Foster) -- Private dancer (Tina Turner) -- Welcome to the pleasuredome (Frankie Goes to Hollywood) -- Hearts on fire (John Cafferty) -- The power of love (Huey Lewis and the News) -- A view to a kill (Duran Duran)
Note: A maxi-single was released for "Welcome to the pleasuredome: the symphonic alternative/Welcome to the pleasuredome: gateway to reality/Brothers in arms" (1986 Zyx 5561, Germany). The title of a subsequent North American release is The Vienna Symphony Project (VSOP). The British release is titled Symphonic rock (1987 Stylus SMR-730, UK).

WARSAW PHILHARMONIC ORCHESTRA

S403 Beatles symphony. 1987 Koch Records International CD-321.645, US (CD).

Contents: Yesterday -- Norwegian wood -- Eleanor Rigby -- Here, there and everywhere -- And I love her -- Fool on the hill -- She's leaving home -- Because -- Across the universe (etc.)
Note: Vadim Brodsky is featured on violin. The orchestra is conducted by Jerzy Sawaroski.

WILSON, JOEMY

S404 Beatles on hammered dulcimer. 1989 Dargason Music DMCD-106, US (CD).

Contents: Eleanor Rigby -- For no one -- When I'm sixty-four -- You've got to hide your love away -- She's leaving home -- Norwegian wood -- And your bird can sing -- In my life -- Eight days a week -- Across the universe -- Yellow submarine -- She loves you
Note: This ensemble of hammered dulcimer, Celtic harp, flute, violin and guitar interprets Beatles' compositions in the style of the Middle Ages/Baroque.

III.

Other Connections Between Rock and the Classics

A. Rock Groups or Artists Recording with Established Orchestras and Choruses

ANDERSON, IAN

see LONDON SYMPHONY ORCHESTRA entries S359 and S364, Part II

ANDERSSON, BENNY

S405 Chess. 1984 RCA CPL2-5340, US/ 1984 RCA PL-70500, UK.

Note: The London Symphony Orchestra and Ambrosian Singers perform with Murray Head, Elaine Paige, and others. The music is composed by Benny Andersson (of Abba) and lyrics are written by Tim Rice and Björn Ulvaeus (of Abba). A single of "One night in Bangkok" by Murray Head was released (1984 RCA 13988, US).

ASHTON, GARDNER & DYKE

S406 The last rebel (film soundtrack). 1971 Capitol SW-827, US.

Note: This film soundtrack was performed by the group Ashton, Gardner & Dyke with the Royal Liverpool Symphony Orchestra. The music was composed by Jon Lord and Tony Ashton.

BATT, MIKE

S407 The hunting of the snark. 1987 Starblend SNARK-1, UK.

Contents: Introduction -- Children of the sky -- The

bellman's speech -- The escapade -- Midnight smoke -- The snooker song -- The pig must die -- The beaver's lesson -- A delicate combination -- As long as the moon can shine -- Dancing towards disaster -- The vanishing
Note: This musical version of Lewis Carroll's nonsense poem features Roger Daltrey, Art Garfunkel, Julian Lennon, Cliff Richard, Deniece Williams, Captain Sensible and the London Symphony Orchestra. It is narrated by Sir John Gielgud and John Hurt.

BLUE NILE

S408 A walk across the rooftops. 1983 A&M SP-6-5087, US/ 1983 Linn LKH-1, UK.

Note: The Blue Nile performs with the string section of the Scottish National Orchestra on several pieces of this album. Although the album was recorded in 1983, it was not released until 1985.

BROOKER, GARY

S409 "The long goodbye." Echoes in the night. 1985 Mercury 824-652-1-M1/ 1985 Mercury MERL-68, UK.

Note: Brooker performs with the National Philharmonic Orchestra on two cuts of this album--one of which is "The long goodbye." Brooker was once a member of the rock group Procol Harum.

ELECTRIC LIGHT ORCHESTRA

S410 Out of the blue. 1977 Jet KZ2-35530, US/ 1977 Jet UAR-100, UK.

Note: The Munich Philharmonic Strings join Electric Light Orchestra on parts of this album. Louis Clark arranged the strings and choir. The album was reissued (1978 Jet/United Artists JT-LA823-L2, US/ 1978 Jet DP-400, UK).

EMERSON, KEITH

S411 "Orchestral suite from Best revenge." Best revenge (film soundtrack). 1986 Chord CHORD-001, UK.

Note: Emerson performs with the National Philharmonic Orchestra on this film soundtrack. This piece also appears on The Emerson collection (1986 Chord CDCOLL-1, UK [CD]).

ESSEX, DAVID

S412 Mutiny! 1983 Mercury MERH-30, UK.

Contents: Overture -- Sailing for a new world -- Setting sail/Sky was clear -- Six weeks late -- Pumpkin -- The lash -- Cape Horn -- Doldrums/Failed Cape Horn -- The letter -- He was born nowhere/Three weeks from paradise -- Land ho -- Tahiti -- Leaving Tahiti -- Observe these men -- Slow we moved -- Captain's table -- Hell -- Mutiny -- Return to England/We prayed for a ship -- Prisoners at the bar -- Bligh's speech -- I'll go no more a-roving -- Finale
Note: David Essex composed the music; he also sings. This musical comedy, based on Mutiny on the Bounty, features the Ambrosian Singers and the Royal Philharmonic Orchestra. Essex also appears on the 1985 London cast recording (1985 Telstar STAR-2261, UK).

FLAIRCK

S413 "Circus." Encore. 1985 EMI 068-127300-1, Netherlands.

Note: Flairck, a Dutch pop group, is accompanied on this 23-minute suite by the North Holland Philharmonic.

FOSTER, DAVID

S414 The symphony sessions. 1988 Atlantic 81799-1, US/ 1988 Atlantic K-781799, UK.

Note: Foster, session player for many rock albums, plays piano with the Vancouver Symphony Orchestra. A videocassette with the same title was released (1987 Atlantic 50120-3, US).

GARFUNKEL, ART

S415 The animals' Christmas. 1986 Columbia FC-40212, US/ 1986 CBS CBS-26704, UK.

Contents: The annunciation -- The creatures of the field -- Just a simple little tune -- The degree -- Incredible Phat -- The friendly beasts -- The song of the camels -- Words from an old Spanish carol -- Carol of the birds -- The frog -- Herod -- Wild geese
Note: Composed by Jimmy Webb, this album features musical performances by Art Garfunkel and Amy Grant with the London Symphony Orchestra.

GIBBONS, STEVE, BAND

S416 "Grace." Down in the bunker. 1978 Polydor PD-1-6154, US/ 1978 Polydor 2391-358, UK.

Note: The London Symphony Orchestra accompanies the Steve Gibbons Band on this rock ballad.

HASLAM, ANNIE

S417 Still life. 1985 Ratpack LCTV-1, UK.

Note: Annie Haslam, a member of the rock group Renaissance, sings with the Royal Philharmonic Orchestra conducted by Louis Clark.

JOHN, ELTON

S418 Elton John live in Australia with the Melbourne Symphony Orchestra. 1987 MCA MCA2-8022, US/ 1988 Rocket/Phonogram EJLP-2, UK.

Contents: Sixty years on -- I need you to turn to -- Greatest discovery -- Tonight -- Sorry seems to be the hardest word -- The king must die -- Take me to the pilot -- Tiny dancer -- Have mercy on the criminal -- Madman across the water -- Candle in the wind -- Burn down the mission -- Your song -- Don't let the sun go down on me
Note: The 88-piece Melbourne Symphony Orchestra performed with Elton John and his 13-piece band only in the last concert of 27 performances in Australia. The live concert was televised to an audience of ten million people on December 14, 1986. The taped version of this concert premiered on Showtime pay TV channel July 11, 1987. A home video with the same title was released (1987 J2 Communications J2-0012, US). For part of the concert Elton John was dressed as a pop Mozart complete with powdered wig. Pictures of him in this attire appear on the front and back covers of the album.

LITTLE RIVER BAND

S419 Backstage pass. 1980 Capitol SWBK-12061, US/ 1980 Capitol 12061, UK.

Relevant contents: It's a long way there -- So many paths -- Statue of liberty -- Fall from paradise -- Light of day -- Reminiscing -- The man in black -- Help is on its way
Note: The Little River Band performs with the Adelaide Symphony Orchestra, conducted by David Measham, on sides one and two of this album. The concert was recorded live at the Adelaide Festival Theatre.

MOODY BLUES

S420 "Isn't life strange?" _Greatest hits_. 1989 Threshold/Polydor 840659-1, US.

Note: This new recording of the song features the London Symphony Orchestra.

S421 "Question." _Greatest hits_. 1989 Threshold/Polydor 840659-1, US.

Note: This new recording of the song features the London Symphony Orchestra.

PAGE, JIMMY

S422 _Death wish II--The original soundtrack_ (film soundtrack). 1982 Swan Song SS-8511, US/ 1982 Swan Song SSK-59415, UK.

Note: Jimmy Page composed music for this film soundtrack and performs on electric guitar and synthesizer with the GLC Philharmonic. A video-cassette of the film _Death wish II_ (1982 Warner Home Video 26032, US) was released.

PARSONS, ALAN, PROJECT

S423 _Pyramid_. 1978 Arista AB-4180, US/ 1978 Arista SPART-1054, UK.

Contents: Voyager -- What goes up -- The eagle will rise again -- One more river -- Can't take it with you -- In the lap of the gods -- Pyramania -- Hyper-gamma-spaces -- Shadow of a lonely man
Note: An unidentified orchestra and the English Chorale appear with Alan Parsons Project on this album.

S424 _Stereotomy_. 1985 Arista AL9-8384, US/ 1985 Arista 207-106, UK.

Contents: Stereotomy -- Beaujolais -- Urbania (instrumental) -- Limelight -- In the real world -- Where's the walrus? (instrumental) -- Light of the world -- Chinese whispers (instrumental) -- Stereotomy two
Note: The Alan Parsons Project with vocalists John Miles, Gary Brooker, Eric Woolfson and others are augmented by the Philharmonia Orchestra. Orchestrations are the work of Andrew Powell. Although not specificly credited on album sleeves/covers, other past and recent Alan Parsons Project albums are reported to have been recorded with the Philharmonia Orchestra.

RICHARD, CLIFF

S425 "All I ask of you/Phantom of the opera overture: act II." 1986 Polydor POSP-802, UK (single). "All I ask of you/Phantom of the opera overture: act III/Only you." 1986 Polydor POSPX-802, UK (12" single).

Note: Cliff Richard and Sarah Brightman are featured in vocals with the Royal Philharmonic Orchestra in these Andrew Lloyd-Webber compositions. Cliff Richard and the Royal Philharmonic Orchestra do not appear on the original London cast album _The phantom of the opera_ (1987 Polygram 831-273-1-Y-2, US/ 1987 Polydor PODV-9, UK). They appear only on this promotional single.

S426 _Dressed for the occasion_. 1986 EMI EMC-3432, UK.

Contents: Green light -- We don't talk anymore -- True love ways -- Softly as I leave you -- Carrie -- Miss you nights -- Galadriel (Spirit of starlight) -- Maybe someday -- Thief in the night -- Up in the world -- Treasure of love -- Devil woman
Note: Cliff Richard performs with the London Philharmonic Orchestra on this album.

RONSTADT, LINDA

S427 _For sentimental reasons_. 1986 Asylum 9-60474-1-E, US/ 1986 Asylum 960474-1 UK.

Contents: When you wish upon a star -- Bewitched, bothered and bewildered -- You go to my head -- But not for me -- My funny valentine -- I get along without you very well -- Am I blue -- I love you for sentimental reasons -- Straighten up and fly right -- Little girl blue -- 'Round midnight
Note: Although these songs are not rock, per se, Linda Ronstadt has often been considered a rock singer. She recorded these nonrock standards with the Nelson Riddle Orchestra.

S428 _Lush life_. 1984 Asylum 60387-1, US/ 1984 Asylum 960387-1, UK.

Contents: When I fall in love -- Skylark -- It never entered my mind -- Mean to me -- When your lover has gone -- I'm a fool to want you -- You took advantage of me -- Sophisticated lady -- Can't we be friends -- My old flame -- Falling in love again -- Lush life
Note: Ronstadt recorded this album with the Nelson Riddle Orchestra.

S429 'Round midnight. 1986 Asylum 9-60489-1-LR, US/ 1986 Asylum 960489-1, UK.

Note: This is a 3 record box set which includes the collective contents of What's new?, For sentimental reasons and Lush life all of which Ronstadt recorded with the Nelson Riddle Orchestra. See 1985 discography for What's new? album information.

SIEGEL, CORKY

S430 "Chamber blues." performed 1988, unreleased.

Note: Siegel on piano, harmonica and vocals teams with Chicago's Consortium String Quartet in a blend of blues and baroque music.

SNOPEK, SIGMUND, III

S431 Roy Rogers meets Albert Einstein. 1982 Mountain Railroad HR-8004, US.

Note: Members of the Milwaukee Symphony Orchestra appear on this rock album. The album was reissued (1988 Dali 20013, US).

TOTO

S432 "Change of heart." Isolation. 1984 Columbia QC-38962, US/ 1984 CBS 86305, UK.

Note: This track features the London Symphony Orchestra.

S433 Dune (film soundtrack). 1984 Polydor 823-770-1-Y-1, US/ 1984 Polydor 823-770-1, UK.

Note: The original score for this soundtrack was composed and performed by members of the rock group Toto. The Vienna Symphony Orchestra and the Vienna Volksoperchoir are featured on this album. A videocassette of the film Dune (1984 Warner Home Video PES-38008; 1985 MCA Home Video VHS-80161, US) was released.

S434 "How does it feel." Isolation. 1984 Columbia QC-38962, US/ 1984 CBS 86305, UK.

Note: This track features the London Symphony Orchestra.

TOWNSHEND, PETE

S435 "Brooklyn kids." _Another scoop_. 1987 Atco 90539-1-G, US/ 1989 Polydor 839-350-1, UK.

Note: Townshend is accompanied by the London Symphony Orchestra on four songs of this album. These previously unreleased pieces were recorded in 1978.

S436 "The ferryman." _Another scoop_. 1987 Atco 90539-1-G, US/ 1989 Polydor 839-350-1, UK.

S437 "Football fugue." _Another scoop_. 1987 Atco 90539-1-G, US/ 1989 Polydor 839-350-1, UK.

S438 "Praying the game." _Another scoop_. 1987 Atco 90539-1-G, US/ 1989 Polydor 839-350-1, UK.

VANGELIS (Vangelis Papathanassiou)

S439 _Heaven and hell_. 1975 RCA Victor AFL1-5110, US/ 1975 RCA RS-1025 (3012), UK.

Note: Jon Anderson is credited for lyrics and lead vocals. The English Chamber Choir provides backup.

VANNELLI, GINO

S440 "Black and blue." _A pauper in paradise_. 1977 A&M SP-4664, US/ 1977 A&M AMLH-64664, UK.

Note: This piece was performed with the Royal Philharmonic Orchestra.

S441 "A pauper in paradise (in four movements)." _A pauper in paradise_. 1977 A&M SP-4664, US/ 1977 A&M AMLH-64664, UK.

Note: This piece was performed with the Royal Philharmonic Orchestra.

WAKEMAN, RICK

S442 "Judas Iscariot." _Criminal record_. 1977 A&M SP-4660, US/ 1977 A&M AMLK-64660, UK.

Note: Wakeman recorded this song with the Ars Laeta Choir of Lausanne, Switzerland.

B. Rock Groups or Artists Appearing with Orchestras in Live Performance before an Audience

Note: An asterisk (*) denotes a performance available as a recorded album (see Part IIIA).

CLAPTON, ERIC

S443 Eric Clapton/National Philharmonic (February 10, 1990), Royal Albert Hall, London

JOHN, ELTON

*S444 Elton John/Melbourne Symphony Orchestra (December 14, 1986), Sydney Entertainment Centre, Sydney

LITTLE RIVER BAND

*S445 Little River Band/Adelaide Symphony Orchestra (1980), Adelaide Festival Theatre, Adelaide

PROCOL HARUM

S446 Procol Harum/Royal Philharmonic Orchestra and Pro Arte Singers (September 22, 1972), Rainbow Theatre, London

STING

S447 Sting/Hamburg State Orchestra (April 1987), Hamburg

WATERS, ROGER

*S448 Roger Waters/East Berlin Rundfunk (Radio) Orchestra & Choir (July 21, 1990), Potsdamer Platz, Berlin

Note: Album details appear in Part IV, "Update," entry 621.

C. Selected Examples of Rock Music Simulating a Baroque or Classical Sound/Structure

ANDERSON, JON

S449 _3 ships_. 1985 Elektra 60469-1, US/ 1985 Elektra EKT-22, UK.

ARBORS

S450 "A symphony for Susan." <u>A symphony for Susan</u>. 1967 Date 3003, US (album); 1966 Date 1529, US (single).

Note: This song, featuring symphonic touches, reached #51 on the Billboard pop chart.

ART OF NOISE

S451 <u>(Who's afraid of?) The Art of Noise!</u> 1984 Island 90179-1, US/ 1984 ZTT ZTTIQ-2, UK.

Note: A <u>Rolling Stone</u> review states that this album has "neo-classical motifs over jazz boogie-woogie bass lines" and uses the musical form "theme and variations."

BLUE JAYS

S452 <u>Blue Jays</u>. 1975 Threshold THS-14, US/ 1975 Threshold THS-1, UK.

Note: The Blue Jays were Justin Hayward and John Lodge of the Moody Blues. This album incorporates cello, piano and violin. A reissue was released (1984 Threshold DOA-8, UK).

BLUNSTONE, COLIN

S453 <u>One year</u>. 1971 Epic KE-30974, US/ 1971 Epic 64557, UK.

Note: This album incorporates a string quartet on many of the tracks.

BOLAN, MARC

(see also T. REX in Part IIIC)

S454 "The wizard." 1966 Decca , UK (single).

Note: This single has full orchestra accompaniment. It also appears on the album <u>T. Rex</u> (1971 Reprise RS-6440, US/ 1970 Fly HIFLY-2, UK) and the compilations <u>Love and death</u> (198? Cherry Red CDBRED-70, UK [CD]), <u>T. Rex</u> (198? Sierra FEDB-5010, UK) and <u>Beyond the rising sun</u> (by the group John's Children) (198? Cambra CR-115, UK). A reissue single was released (1982 Cherry Red CHERRY-39, UK).

BOWIE, DAVID

(see also Part I)

S455 "The wild-eyed boy from Freecloud." <u>Man of words, man of music</u>. 1969 Mercury ST-61246, US/ 1969 Philips SBL-7912, UK.

Note: This song features orchestral accompaniment. The album was reissued as <u>Space oddity</u> (1972 RCA Victor LSP-4813, US and 19?? RCA AQL1-4813, US). An alternate version with cello and acoustic guitar appears on the B-side of the single "Space oddity" (1969 Mercury 72949, US/ 1969 Philips 1081, UK), on a track of the bootleg album <u>Changesthree</u> (1983 Grace AZL1-1984, US), and on a track of the compilation <u>Sound + Vision</u> (1989 Rykodisc RALP-00120/21/22, US).

CHAD AND JEREMY

S456 "The progress suite." <u>Of cabbages and kings</u>. 1967 Columbia CL-2671 (mono), CS-9471 (stereo), US.

Note: Both vocal and instrumental sections are included in this five-part suite. The parts are entitled: Prologue; Decline; Editorial; Fall; Epilogue.

DEAD CAN DANCE

S457 <u>Within the realm of a dying sun</u>. 1987 4AD CAD-705, UK.

Note: On this album the group Dead Can Dance blends the unusual rock instrumentation of violins, viola, cellos, trumpet, trombones, bass trombone, oboe, timpani, and military snare.

DEEP PURPLE

(see also Part I)

S458 "Burn." <u>Burn</u>. 1974 Warner Bros. W-2766, US/ 1974 Purple TPS-3505, UK.

Note: This piece includes baroque-like organ breaks. It also appears on the compilations <u>When we rock, we rock and when we roll, we roll</u> (1978 Warner Bros. PRK-3223, US) and <u>Deepest purple</u> (1980 Warner Bros. PRK-3486, US/ 1980 Harvest EMITV-25, UK). Live versions appear on <u>Made in Europe</u> (1976 Warner Bros. PR-2995, US/ 1976 Purple TPSA-7517, UK) and <u>Live in London</u> (1982 Harvest SHSP-4124, UK).

DOLBY, THOMAS

(see also Part I)

S459 Music from the film Gothic (film soundtrack). 1987 Virgin 90607-1, US/ 1987 Virgin V-2417, UK.

Note: Dolby uses a baroque harpsichord style and Gregorian choirs. The score is mainly synthesized with occasional orchestral interludes and allusions to the styles of Stravinsky, Vaughan Williams, and Bartók. The Stravinsky quotes scattered throughout the score seem to be derived from sampling. A videocassette of the film Gothic (1987 Vestron Video 5215, US) was released.

DOWNES, GEOFFREY/THE NEW DANCE ORCHESTRA

S460 The light program(me). 1987 Geffen GHS-24156, US/ 1987 Geffen K-924156-1, UK.

Note: Downes, a member of the rock group Asia, recorded this all-instrumental double album on various synthesizers. Although Downes is the sole performer, the series of thirty tracks sounds orchestral.

EINSTEIN

S461 First principles. 1979 WEA 58060, Germany.

Note: This German band presents "pomp rock" similar to that of Saga; Emerson, Lake & Palmer; and Kansas.

ELECTRIC STRING BAND

S462 "Say you don't mind." 1967 Deram DM-122, UK (single).

Note: Denny Laine is backed by amplified string quartet on this single. A reissue was released (1969 Deram DM-227, UK). The song was copied in 1971 by Colin Blunstone (1971 Epic EPC-7765, UK [single]; One year 1971 Epic KE-30974, US/ 1971 Epic 64557, UK [albums]). The original version appears on the compilation Deram dayze (1987 Decal/Charly LIK-9, UK).

EMERSON, KEITH

S463 "Bach before the mast." Honky. 198? Cinevox Spa, Italy.

Note: This piece is the traditional "Sailor's hornpipe" performed in the style of J. S. Bach as written by George Malcolm. It also appears on The Emerson collection (1986 Chord CDCOLL-1, UK [CD]).

FEVER TREE

(see also Part I)

S464 <u>Fever tree</u>. 1968 Uni 73024, 19?? MCA 551, US/ 1968 Uni UNLS-102, UK.

Note: This album integrates piano, organ, harp, flute, bass recorder, clavinette, harpsichord, cello, strings, horns, guitars and drums. Baroque-like sounds are heard on "Filigree and shadow," "The sun also rises," and a version of the Beatles' "Day-tripper/We can work it out." "Filigree and shadow" was released as a single (1969 Uni 55146, US).

FOGELBERG, DAN

S465 "Nether lands." <u>Nether lands</u>. 1977 Epic PE-34185, US/ 1977 Epic 81574, UK.

Note: This song features an orchestral arrangement.

FOREIGNER

S466 "Starrider." <u>Foreigner</u>. 1977 Atlantic SD-18215 (19109), US/ 1977 Atlantic K-50356, UK.

Note: This piece incorporates harpsichord-like effects.

GRASS ROOTS

S467 "Bella Linda." <u>Feelings</u>. 1968 Dunhill 50027, US (album); 1968 Dunhill 4162, US (single).

Note: This song features a string section and harp. The single was reissued (1968 Dunhill 1435, US). It also appears on the compilation albums <u>Golden grass</u> (1969 Dunhill DS-50047, US), <u>Their 16 greatest hits</u> (1971 Dunhill DS-50107; 1980 MCA MCA-37154, US), <u>Temptation eyes</u> (1985 MCA MCA-20194, US), and <u>The Grass Roots' greatest hits, volume 1</u> (1987 MCA MCA-31132, US).

HENRY COW

S468 <u>Legend</u>. 1973 Virgin VR13-107, US/ 1973 Virgin V-2005, UK.

Note: Fred Frith and Dagmar Krause are members of this group. Their music shows classical influences of Stockhausen, Varèse and Weill.

HUGO LARGO

S469 _Drum_. 1987 Relativity 88561-8167-1, US/ 1988 Land LAND-02, UK.

Note: The group Hugo Largo features two bass guitars, violin and a vocalist. Two members are Glenn Branca alumni. This album was reissued (1988 Opal 25768, US) in a remixed version plus two additional tracks.

JACKSON, JOE

S470 _Will power_. 1987 A&M SP-3908, US/ 1987 A&M AMA-3908, UK.

Note: This all-instrumental album ranges from solo piano on "Nocturne" to "Symphony in one movement" with winds, drums, orchestral percussion, sax, guitar, synthesizer and thirty-four strings.

JAM

S471 "Smithers-Jones." _Setting sons_. 1979 Polydor PD-1-6249, US/ 1979 Polydor POLD-5018 (2442-168), UK.

Note: The predominant musical setting for this song sounds like a string quartet. This song also appears on the compilation album _Snap!_ (1983 Polydor 422-815-537-1-Y-2, US/ 1983 Snap SNAP-1, UK).

LAIBACH

S472 _Let it be_. 1988 Enigma 7-75404-1, US/ 1988 Mute STUMM-58, UK.

Note: Songs from the Beatles' album _Let it be_ are interpreted in an operatic style by this Yugoslavian rock band.

LOVE

S473 _Forever changes_. 1967 Elektra EKS-74013, US/ 1971 Elektra K-42015, UK.

Note: The strings added to selections on this album create a neo-classical effect.

McCARTNEY, PAUL

S474 _Give my regards to Broad Street_ (film soundtrack). 1984 MPL SC-39613, US/ 1984 Parlophone EL-260278-1, UK.

Note: Produced by George Martin, this album includes orchestration for a string quartet which accompanies McCartney on remakes of the Beatles' songs "Eleanor Rigby" and "For no one." A videocassette of the film Give my regards to Broad Street (1985 CBS/Fox Video VHS-1448, US) was released.

S475 "Junk." McCartney. 1970 Apple/Capitol STAO/SMAS-3363, US/ 1970 Apple 7102, UK.

Note: This is a short song performed in a waltz-like rhythm. The album was reissued (1979 Columbia PC(JC)-36478, US).

MORAZ, PATRICK

S476 "Modular symphony (1st movement)." Human interface. 1987 Cinema/Capitol ST-12558, US/ 1987 Capitol EST-2043, UK.

Note: This piece is classically styled synthesizer music.

MORRISON, VAN

S477 "Snow in San Anselmo." Hard nose the highway. 1973 Warner Bros. BS-2712, US/ 1973 Warner Bros. K-46242, UK.

Note: A studio choir lends a classical tinge to this song.

ORDINAIRES

S478 One. 1989 Bar None/Restless 72615-1, US/ 1990 Brave/One Little Indian BND-7LP, UK.

S479 The Ordinaires. 1990 Bar None/Restless 72632-2, US (CD)/ 1985 Dossier ST-7509, Germany/ 1987 Zoar

Note: This group is a nine-piece chamber rock group with two violins, one cello, electric guitars, bass, saxophones and drums.

PARZIVAL

S480 Ba-rock. 197? Teldec 14685, Germany.

PENGUIN CAFÉ ORCHESTRA

S481 Broadcasting from home. 1984 Editions EG EGED-38, US and UK.

PINK FLOYD

S482 A saucerful of secrets. 1968 Tower ST-5131, US/ 1968 Columbia SCX-6258, UK.

Note: This album has been described as one that takes sonics of the avant-garde and applies them to classical music structures.

S483 "Summer 68." Atom heart mother. 1970 Harvest SMAS-382, US/ 1970 Harvest SHVL-781, UK.

Note: This song includes a brass choir and piano.

PRINCE

S484 "Pop life." Around the world in a day. 1985 Paisley Park/Warner Bros. 25286-1, US/ 1985 Warner Bros. 925286-1, UK.

Note: This piece includes a string interlude.

S485 "Raspberry beret." Around the world in a day. 1985 Paisley Park/Warner Bros. 25286-1, US/ 1985 Warner Bros. 925286-1, UK.

Note: This piece incorporates cello and violin.

PROCOL HARUM

S486 Grand hotel. 1973 Chrysalis CHR-1037, US and UK.

Note: Parts of this album are backed by an orchestra and choir.

REVERE, PAUL, AND THE RAIDERS

S487 "Undecided man." The spirit of '67. 1967 Columbia CL-2595 (mono), CS-9395 (stereo), US.

Note: A string quartet creates an orchestral effect on this song.

SAGITTARIUS

S488 "My world fell down." Present tense. 1968 Columbia CS-9644, US (album); 1967 Columbia 4-44163, US (single).

Note: This piece sounds like the music of a string quartet.

SHELLEYAN ORPHAN

S489 Helleborine. 1987 Columbia BFC-40545, US/ 1987 Rough Trade ROUGH-97, UK.

Note: The songs on this recording are played by a string trio accompanied by woodwinds, acoustic guitar, and harp.

SIOUXSIE AND THE BANSHEES

S490 "Dazzle." Hyaena. 1984 Geffen GHS-24030, US/ 1984 Wonderland SHEHP-1, UK; 198? Polydor 821-510-1.

Note: The introduction to this song includes an orchestral string section. There is also a 12" single "glamour" mix of this song (1984 Wonderland SHEX, UK) and a 7" single (1984 Wonderland SHE7, UK).

S491 The thorn. 1984 Geffen 881396-1, US/ 1984 Wonderland SHEEP-8, UK (EP).

Note: A forty-seven piece string section appears on this EP.

SPOOKY TOOTH

S492 Ceremony. 1969 A&M SP-4225, US/ 1969 Island ILPS-9107, UK.

Note: This album is an electronic mass written by French avant-gardist Pierre Henry and Gary Wright of Spooky Tooth.

SQUIRE, CHRIS

S493 Fish out of water. 1975 Atlantic SD-18159, US/ 1975 Atlantic K-50203, UK.

Note: This solo album by Chris Squire of Yes is complemented by a studio orchestra. The parts were orchestrated by Andrew Pryce Jackman.

T. REX

(see also BOLAN, MARC in Part IIIC)

S494 "Cosmic dancer." Electric warrior. 1971 Warner Bros. RS-6466, US/ 1971 Fly HIFLY-6, UK.

Note: This song composed by Marc Bolan includes what sounds like a string quartet.

TALK TALK

S495 Spirit of Eden. 1988 EMI/Manhattan E1-46977, US/ 1988 Parlophone PCSD-105, UK.

Note: Violins, woodwinds and trumpet lend a chamber music-like sound to this album. The Chelmsford Cathedral Choir appears on "I believe in you."

10,000 MANIACS

S496 "Verdi cries." In my tribe. 1987 Elektra 60738-1, US/ 1987 Elektra EKT-41, UK.

THIS MORTAL COIL

S497 "Kangaroo." It'll end in tears. 1984 Valentino 90269-1, US/ 1984 4AD CAD-411, UK.

TOWNSHEND, PETE

(see also Part IIIA)

S498 "Baroque ippanese." Another scoop. 1987 Atco 90539-1-G, US/ 1989 Polydor 839-350-1, UK.

S499 "Prelude #556." Another scoop. 1987 Atco 90539-1-G, US/ 1989 Polydor 839-350-1, UK.

TWELFTH NIGHT

S500 Art and illusion. 1984 Music for Nations MFN-36, UK.

S501 Fact and fiction. 1983 Twelfth Night TN-006, UK.

WAY, DARRYL, WITH OPUS 20

S502 The human condition. 1988 Virgin 7-90657-1, US/ 1987 Venture VE-8, UK.

Note: This album is a suite for string orchestra, piano and percussion. Darryl Way was once a member of the rock group Curved Air.

D. Rock Music Influences on Classical Music

1. Classical Composers

ADAMS, JOHN

S503 Nixon in China. c1987, 1988 Elektra/Nonesuch 79177-1, US/ 1988 Nonesuch 979-177-1, UK.

Note: Adams' opera combines minimalism and romanticism synthesized with popular traditions including rock. Some of the arias employ the musical beat and rhythmic structure of a rock song. Selections from the opera were released on Music from Nixon in China (1988 Elektra/Nonesuch 79193-1, US).

ASHLEY, ROBERT

S504 Perfect lives (Private parts): The lessons. 1981 Lovely Music/Vital Records VR-4908, US.

Note: Twenty-eight one-minute pieces for television are derived from songs heard in "The bank (episode three)" of Perfect lives/Private parts, an opera in seven episodes for television (1983 Lovely Music LMC-4913, 4947, US [cassettes]).

BERNSTEIN, LEONARD

S505 Mass. 1972 Columbia M2-31008, US/ 1972 CBS 77256, UK.

Note: This work created for the opening of the John F. Kennedy Center for the Performing Arts includes the traditional orchestra as well as electric guitars and keyboards.

BRANCA, GLENN

S506 Symphony no. 6: Devil chorus at the gates of heaven. 1989 Blast First 7-71426-1, UK.

Note: This symphony was composed for guitars, electric keyboard and drums.

JOHNSON, SCOTT

S507 Bird in the domes. unreleased.

Note: This string quartet music disguises a Chuck Berry riff according to the composer.

S508 John Somebody. 1986 Nonesuch 79133, US.

Contents: John Somebody -- No memory

Note: Johnson is a crossover composer who writes modern classical music with some rock instrumentation and riffs interspersed in classical structures. His early music experience was with electric guitar.

ROUSE, CHRISTOPHER

S509 "Bump." Symphony no. 1; phantasmata. 1989 Nonesuch 79230-2, US (CD).

Note: Composer Christopher Rouse says that this symphonic piece, recorded by the Baltimore Symphony Orchestra, includes subtle quotes from Led Zeppelin and Canned Heat rock music.

2. Classical Record Packaging

FOX, VIRGIL

S510 Heavy organ at Carnegie Hall, vol. 2. 1974 RCA Red Seal ARL1-0477, US.

VARIOUS ORCHESTRAS

S511 The baroque juke box. 1989 CBS Records Masterworks MGT-44672, US (cassette).

S512 Chopin hit parade. 1969 Philips PHS-900-230/231 (SPS-2-908), US.

S513 The classical jukebox. 1989 CBS Records Masterworks MGT-44670 and 44671, US (cassette).

S514 The opera juke box. 1989 CBS Records Masterworks MGT-44673, US (cassette).

S515 Pachelbel's greatest hit. 1984 RCA Red Seal MRL1-8523, US.

Note: This album features six arrangements of "Canon in D major."

3. Rock Artists Appearing in Straight Classical Roles and/or Collaborating with Classical Composers/Performers

ANDERSON, IAN

S516 "The water's edge." 1979 unreleased.

Note: This music composed by Ian Anderson and

Martin Barre (both of Jethro Tull) in collaboration with David Palmer was performed by the Orchestra of the Scottish Ballet. A ballet of the same title is choreographed to the music. The ballet was performed originally as part of "Underground rumours" in 1979. It has been performed several times since then in the 1980s. Another version is arranged for piano by David Palmer.

ANDERSON, JON

S517 "Ursprung." 1979 unreleased.

Note: This music composed by Jon Anderson (of Yes) was performed by the Orchestra of the Scottish Ballet for a ballet of the same title. The ballet was performed originally as part of "Underground rumours" in 1979. It has been performed several times since then in the 1980s. An unreleased synthesized tape version was also made by Jon Anderson.

ANDERSON, LAURIE

S518 "Forgetting." Songs from liquid days. 1986 CBS FM-39564, US and UK.

Note: Laurie Anderson wrote the lyrics for this song in collaboration with Philip Glass who composed the music. The vocals are performed by Linda Ronstadt backed by the Roches and the Kronos String Quartet.

BOWIE, DAVID

S519 "The drowned girl." David Bowie in Bertolt Brecht's Baal. 1982 RCA Victor CPL1-4346, US/ 1982 RCA BOW-11, UK (EP).

Note: David Bowie performs this Brecht/Weill song in a BBC-TV production. The song originally was part of Kurt Weill's "Das Berliner requiem."

BYRNE, DAVID

S520 "Liquid days (part one)." Songs from liquid days. 1986 CBS FM-39564, US and UK.

Note: David Byrne wrote the lyrics for this song in collaboration with Philip Glass who composed the music. The Roches perform the vocals.

S521 Music for The knee plays. 1985 ECM 25022-1, US/ 1985 Zonophone EJ-240381-1, UK.

Contents: Tree (Today is an important occasion) -- In the upper room -- The sound of business -- Social studies -- (The gift of sound) Where the sun never goes down -- Theadora is dozing -- Admiral Perry -- I bid you goodnight -- I've tried -- Winter -- Jungle book -- In the future

Note: This music was composed for use as short connecting passages between the scenes of Robert Wilson's opera "The civil wars." The classically structured pieces draw on the brass sound of New Orleans processional bands. These pieces were recorded in early April 1984 and performed for the first time live on April 26-28, 1984 at the Walker Art Center, Minneapolis, Minnesota.

S522 "Open the kingdom (Liquid days part two)." Songs from liquid days. 1986 CBS FM-39564, US and UK.

Note: David Byrne wrote the lyrics for this song in collaboration with Philip Glass who composed the music. Douglas Perry performs the vocals.

CALE, JOHN

S523 "The Falklands suite." Words for the dying. 1989 Opal 9-26024-1, US/ 1989 Land LAND-09, UK.

Note: This suite comprises four Dylan Thomas poems and three interludes all scored for chamber orchestra, pedal steel guitar and children's choir. On the album this suite was performed by the Orchestra of Symphonic and Popular Music of Gosteleradio USSR and the Choir of Llandaf Cathedral Choir School, South Wales. Its 1987 world debut was performed by the Metropole Orchestra on Dutch television. The American première was in early 1988 with Cale at the piano.

S524 Sanctus. November 1987 unrecorded.

Note: This music was commissioned by the Randy Warshaw Dance Company. Kurzweils and string synthesizers were utilized.

COPELAND, STEWART

S525 Holy blood and crescent moon. 1989 unreleased.

Note: Copeland is a drummer for the rock group Police. This opera was performed by the Cleveland Opera premièring October 10-15, 1989 at the State Theater, Cleveland, Ohio. The subject matter has to do with the Crusades.

S526 Lear. April 16-21, 1985 unreleased.

Note: Copeland composed this score for the San Francisco Ballet interpretation of "King Lear." This modern ballet using classical technique premièred at San Francisco's War Memorial Opera House.

DALTREY, ROGER

S527 Mack the knife (film soundtrack). 1989 CBS SM-45630, US.

Note: Daltrey, well-known singer of the rock group Who, stars as the street singer in a film version of Kurt Weill's The threepenny opera. He has recorded four songs. A home video version of the film Mack the knife (1990 RCA/Columbia Pictures Home Video 77003, US) was released.

DAVIES, IVA

S528 Boxes. 1988 Chrysalis VK-41659, US (CD).

Note: Iva Davies and Bob Kretschmer, of the Australian rock band Icehouse, composed this avant-garde ballet score which premièred at the Sydney Opera House. Surrealist Jean Cocteau is the subject of the ballet. A videocassette is available in Australia. Iva Davies is a classically-trained oboist who once played with the Sydney Symphony.

EMERSON, KEITH

S529 Works, volume 1. 1977 Atlantic SD2-7000, US/ 1977 Manticore K-80009, UK.

Note: The photograph of Keith Emerson on the inside of this Emerson, Lake & Palmer album shows him in the same pose as a famous photograph of Igor Stravinsky.

FALL

S530 I am kurious oranj. 1988 Beggars Banquet/RCA 9582-1-H, US/ 1988 Beggars Banquet BEGA-96, UK.

Note: This music is the original score composed for the ballet "I am curious orange" performed by Michael Clark and Company. The subject is William of Orange. This ballet premièred in Amsterdam June 11, 1988 and was later performed at Edinburgh and Sadler's Wells Theatre in London. According to liner notes, this collaboration marks the first time a rock group has played music live for the ballet.

LLOYD-WEBBER, ANDREW

S531 Requiem. 1985 Angel DFO-1-38218, US/ 1985 His Master's Voice/EMI EL-270242-1, UK.

Contents: Requiem & Kyrie -- Dies Irae --

Offertorium -- Hosanna -- Pie Jesu --
Lux aeterna & Libera me
Note: This formal requiem is performed by the English Chamber Orchestra, Winchester Cathedral Choir, Plácido Domingo (tenor), Sarah Brightman (soprano) and Paul Miles-Kingston (treble). The lyrics are sung in Latin. A single of "Pie Jesu" (1985 Angel 5467, US/ 1985 HMV , UK) reached the top ten on the UK pop chart. A video of this single was also released. A live performance of the requiem appeared on television during the Easter season in 1985 (BBC in UK/PBS in US). A videocassette Requiem (1986 Kultur 1132, US) is available.

PENDARVIS, JANICE

see Suzanne Vega S538

ROCHES

see Laurie Anderson S518
see David Byrne S521

RONSTADT, LINDA

see Laurie Anderson S518
see Suzanne Vega S537

SIMON, PAUL

S532 "Changing opinion." Songs from liquid days. 1986 CBS FM-39564, US and UK.

Note: Paul Simon wrote the lyrics for this song in collaboration with Philip Glass who composed the music. Vocals are performed by Bernard Fowler.

SNOPEK, SIGMUND, III

S533 Orange blue. composed 1969/performed 1972, unrecorded.

Note: Rock musician Snopek composed this symphony for the Milwaukee Symphony Orchestra.

S534 Talking symphony. 1975 unrecorded.

STING

S535 The soldier's tale. 1988 Pangaea PAN-6233, US/ 1988 Pangaea PEA-461-048-1, UK.

Note: This version of Igor Stravinsky's work features several musicians and three actors including Sting as the Soldier, Vanessa Redgrave as the Devil and Ian McKellen as the Narrator. Kent Nagano conducts members of the London Sinfonietta.

S536 3 penny opera. 1990 A&M ?

Note: Sting performs the part of MacHeath and Maureen McGovern plays Polly Peachum. This stage version of Kurt Weill's work opened at the National Theatre, Washington, D.C. (September and October 1989) and on Broadway, New York, N.Y. (November and December 1989).

VEGA, SUZANNE

S537 "Freezing." Songs from liquid days. 1986 CBS FM-39564, US and UK.

Note: Suzanne Vega wrote the lyrics for this song in collaboration with Philip Glass who composed the music. Vocals are performed by Linda Ronstadt backed by the Kronos String Quartet.

S538 "Lightning." Songs from liquid days. 1986 CBS FM-39564, US and UK.

Note: Suzanne Vega wrote the lyrics for this song in collaboration with Philip Glass who composed the music. Vocals are performed by Janice Pendarvis who has previously appeared as a backup singer for Sting.

ZAPPA, FRANK

S539 The Varèse record. 1977 Finnadar SR-9018, US.

Note: Some of the program notes for this classical album were written by Frank Zappa, a fan of Edgard Varèse.

4. Classical Composers, Conductors and Performers in Rock Roles

BOYD, LIONA

S540 Persona. 1986 CBS FM-42120, US and UK.

Contents: L'enfant -- Sun child -- Memories of a thousand moons -- Sorceress -- Mother and sister -- Labyrinth -- Phoenix reborn -- Sea of tranquility -- Destiny -- Flight of the phoenix -- Persona
Note: Boyd, a classical guitarist, plays music written or arranged by rock artists and produced by Michael Kamen. David Gilmour, Eric Clapton and Michael Kamen make cameo appearances with Boyd on various pieces. Gilmour plays an electric guitar

solo on "Persona," Clapton plays electric guitar on "Labyrinth" and Kamen plays various instruments throughout the contents of the album.

CABALLÉ, MONTSERRAT

S541 Barcelona. 1988 Polydor POLH-44, UK.

Note: Opera star Caballé guests on this album composed and performed by Freddie Mercury (of Queen). Singles were released for "Barcelona" (1987 Polydor POSP-887 [7"single]; POSPX-887 [12" single], UK) and "The golden boy" (1988 Polydor PO-23 [7" single]; PZ-23 [12" single], UK). The single "Barcelona" reached #8 on the UK pop singles chart.

GLASS, PHILIP

S542 "The answer." The sky and the ground. 1989 Beggars Banquet 9636-1-H, US/ 1988 Beggars Banquet BEGA-97, UK.

Note: Pierce Turner collaborates with Philip Glass on this piece. Turner composed and performed the work; Glass added oboe and cello arrangements.

S543 Carmina burana. 1983 A&M SP-4945, US/ 1983 A&M AMLX-64945, UK.

Note: Philip Glass produced Ray Manzarek's rock version of Orff's "Carmina burana."

S544 Changing hearts. 1981 RCA AFL1-4043, US/ 1981 RCA PL- , UK.

Note: This album performed by the rock group Polyrock was produced by Philip Glass.

S545 It's only a long way across. 1987 Beggars Banquet 6698-1-H, US/ 1986 Beggars Banquet BEGA-77, UK.

Note: This rock album performed by Pierce Turner was produced by Philip Glass.

S546 "The late great Johnny Ace." Hearts and bones. 1983 Warner Bros. 1-23942, US/ 1983 Warner Bros. 92-3942-1, UK.

Note: Glass scored the classical chamber orchestra coda for Paul Simon's rock song "The late great Johnny Ace."

S547 Polyrock. 1980 RCA AFL1-3714, US/ 1980 RCA PL-43502, UK.

Note: Philip Glass produced this album which was

performed by the rock group Polyrock.

SCHOENER, EBERHARD

S548 Video-magic. 1981 Harvest ST-12171, US/ 1978 Harvest 45234, Europe.

Contents: Trans-Am -- Why don't you answer -- Natural high -- Signs of emotion -- Flashback -- Octagon -- San Francisco waitress -- Code-word Elvis -- Powerslide
Note: Eberhard Schoener composed the words and music for these rock songs. Schoener on keyboards and synthesizer is joined by Sting on vocals and bass, Andy Summers on guitar, Stewart Copeland on drums and others. A compilation of this album and Flashback (1978 Harvest 32839, Europe) was released as Video flashback (1979 Harvest SHSM-2030, UK). A more recent compilation is titled Music from Video magic and Flashback (1987 GAIA 13-9003-1, US).

(see also Schoener's role as conductor in 1985 discography Part IIIA, entries 604 and 605)

IV.

Update to Parts I, II, III and Appendixes of 1985 Discography

Note: Part IV, "Update," includes updated information, expanded detail unknown at the time of the original discography and minor corrections for entries of Rockin' the Classics and Classicizin' the Rock (Greenwood Press, 1985). Entry numbers in this part correlate with specific entry numbers in the 1985 discography. Instructions are given in uppercase print followed by a colon.

I.
ROCKIN' THE CLASSICS

ANIMALS

002 REVISE ANIMAL TRACKS US ALBUM INFORMATION:
1965 MGM E-4305 (mono), 1965 MGM SE-4305 (stereo), US

REVISE THE BEST OF THE ANIMALS ALBUM INFORMATION IN NOTE:
1966 MGM E-4324 (mono), 1966 MGM SE-4324 (stereo), US

ADD AT END OF NOTE:
The best of the Animals was reissued again (1987 Abkco 4324-1, US). This song also appears on Greatest hits live! (1984 I.R.S. SP-70043, US/ 1984 I.R.S. IRSA-7043, UK).

APOLLO 100

004 CORRECT ALBUM RELEASE YEAR ON ENTRIES 004-012 AND 014-017:
198? = 1981

005 ADD UK ALBUM INFORMATION:
/ 1973 CBS/Youngblood SSYB-3005, UK.

006 REVISE SPELLING IN NOTE:
Danse = Dance

007 DELETE ENTRY BECAUSE SOURCE IS NOT CLASSICAL.

014 ADD SOURCE INFORMATION:
Source: Beethoven/Sonata no. 8 in C minor, op. 13

BEATLES

039 ADD TO ENTRY AFTER 1974 CAPITOL ALBUM NUMBER 5964:
(6300)

041 ADD TO ENTRY AFTER 1964 CAPITOL ALBUM NUMBER 5112:
(6278)

BENNINGHOFF'S BAD ROCK BLUES BAND

045 ADD SSS- PREFIX TO ALBUM NUMBER ON ENTRIES 045-048 AND 053-056.

049 DELETE ENTIRE ENTRY BECAUSE SOURCE IS NOT CLASSICAL.

050 ADD SSS- PREFIX TO ALBUM NUMBER ON ENTRIES 050-052.

BLOOD, SWEAT & TEARS

057 ADD AT END OF SOURCE AFTER OP. 60:
, mvt. 2, first theme, Romance

BUMBLE, B., AND THE STINGERS

060 ADD TO NOTE BEFORE SEE ALSO:
This instrumental also appears on the compilation Instrumental rock (1986 Music for Pleasure MFP-415750-1, UK).

061 ADD TO NOTE BEFORE SEE ALSO:
This instrumental also appears on the compilations Wipeout--20 instrumental greats (1986 Impression LPIMP-5, UK), 20 one hit wonders, vol. 1 (1986 See for Miles CM-111, UK), and The history of rock instrumentals, vol. 1 (1987 Rhino RNLP-70137, US and UK).

CARLOS, WALTER (WENDY)

065 ADD UK ALBUM INFORMATION:
/ 1969 CBS ,UK.

ADD AFTER SECOND SENTENCE IN NOTE:
Note: This was the first "classical" album in ten years to win a "gold record."

CARMEN, ERIC

095 ADD AT END OF NOTE:
Reissues of the album (1982 Fame FA-3049, UK) and single (198? Old Gold OG-9122, UK) were released. "All by myself" also appears on the compilation The best of Eric Carmen (1988 Arista AL-8547, US/ 1989 Arista 20899, UK).

COUGARS

100 ADD AT END OF NOTE:
This instrumental also appears on the compilations Instrumental rock (1986 Music for Pleasure MFP-415750-1, UK) and 20 one hit wonders, vol. 1 (1986 See for Miles CM-111, UK).

CURVED AIR

102 ADD TO NOTE AFTER FIRST SENTENCE:
"Vivaldi" also appears on The best of Curved Air (1976 Warner Bros. K-36015, UK).

DANNA, MYCHAEL

103 ADD ALBUM INFORMATION AND CONTENTS:
1980 F. Harris Music Co. FHR-803, US.

Contents: Prelude in C# minor (Rachmaninoff) -- Dance of the blessed spirits [from Orpheus] (Gluck) -- March #1 [from Floridante] (Handel) -- March #2 [from Floridante] (Handel) -- Canon in D major (Pachelbel) -- Minute waltz [op. 64, no. 1] (Chopin) -- Largo [from Serse] (Handel) -- Toccata in D minor [BWV 565] (J. S. Bach) -- Fugue in D minor [BWV 565] (J. S. Bach)

DEEP PURPLE

104 ADD AT END OF NOTE:
This album was reissued (1988 Passport PB-3607, US).

DEODATO (Emir Deodato)

(see also ADDENDA page 74 in 1985 discography)

105 ADD AT END OF NOTE:
"Also sprach Zarathustra" also appears on Best of Deodato (198? IMS 813-660-2, UK (CD) and Live at Felt Forum (1989 CBS Associated ZK45221, US [CD]).

107 ADD NOTE:
Note: "Pavane for a dead princess" also appears on Best of Deodato (198? IMS 813-660-2, UK [CD]).

108 ADD NOTE:
Note: "Prelude to afternoon of a faun" also appears on Best of Deodato (198? IMS 813-660-2, UK [CD]).

109 ADD AT END OF NOTE:
"Rhapsody in blue" also appears on Best of Deodato (198? IMS 813-660-2, UK [CD]).

EKSEPTION

131 ADD INFORMATION ABOUT SINGLE:
; 1969 Fontana F-1655, US (single).

REVISE SOURCE:
Beethoven/Symphony no. 5 in C minor, op. 67, mvt. 1; Sonata no. 14 in C sharp minor, op. 27, no. 2 (Moonlight Sonata); and Piano Sonata no. 1 in F minor, op. 2, no. 1

135 REVISE SOURCE:
Beethoven/Symphony no. 5 in C minor, op. 67

147 ADD INFORMATION ABOUT SINGLE:
; 1969 Fontana F-1655, US (single).

ELECTRIC LIGHT ORCHESTRA

156 ADD AT END OF NOTE:
It also appears on the compilation album The light shines on (1977 Harvest SHSM-2015, UK).

ELECTROPHON

157 REVISE ALBUM RELEASE DATE ON ENTRIES 157-167:
1977 = 1975

ADD SOURCE INFORMATION:
Source: Mozart

166 ADD SOURCE INFORMATION:
Source: Schubert

EMERSON, LAKE & PALMER

181 ADD TO NOTE AFTER THE SENTENCE THAT ENDS WITH "IN THE U.S. IN 1975":
A videocassette Emerson, Lake & Palmer in Lindsay Clennell's production of Pictures at an exhibition is available (1984 Classic Family Entertainment G153, UK).

ADD AT END OF NOTE:
A half-speed mastered reissue was released (1979 Mobile Fidelity Sound Lab MFSL-1-031, US).

ENO, BRIAN

183 ADD NOTE:
Note: This album is also part of the box set _Working backwards, 1983-1973_ (1983 Editions EG EGBS-2, US and UK).

FOGELBERG, DAN

197 ADD AT END OF NOTE:
/ 1982 Epic EPC-32653, UK).

FOUR SEASONS

198 ADD AT END OF NOTE:
and _25th anniversary collection_ (1987 Rhino RNRP-72998, US) and _The 20 greatest hits of Frankie Valli & the Four Seasons live_ (1989 MCA/Curb CRBD-10900, US [CD]).

JETHRO TULL

224 AT BEGINNING OF NOTE DELETE COMMA AFTER "THE ALBUM".

ADD AT END OF NOTE:
and also on the compilation _Living in the past_ (1972 Chrysalis 2CH-1035 [2TS-2106], US/ 1972 Chrysalis CJT-1, UK). Another version of this instrumental featuring Ian Anderson with the London Symphony Orchestra appears on _A classic case--the London Symphony Orchestra plays the music of Jethro Tull featuring Ian Anderson_ (1985 RCA Red Seal XRL1-7067, US/ 1986 RCA RL-71134, UK). An acoustic version is included in the box set _20 years of Jethro Tull_ (1988 Chrysalis V5X-41653, US/ 1988 Chrysalis TBOX-1, UK).

KAZDIN, ANDREW (with Thomas Z. Shepard)

228 REVISE ALBUM RELEASE DATE ON ENTRIES 228-231:
197? = 1971

ADD NOTE:
Note: This piece is also on side 2 of _Bolero_ (1978 CBS Masterworks -7117; reissued 1980 CBS Masterworks MX-35860, US).

LLOYD-WEBBER, ANDREW

241 ADD AFTER ALBUM TITLE:
1977 MCA MCA-2332;

REVISE NOTE:
Note: Andrew's brother Julian plays cello on this piece. There are 23 variations on the album. A single "Theme and variations: Variation 16/

Variations 1-4" was released (1978 MCA MCA-40866, US/ 1978 MCA MCA-345, UK). "Variation 5/Variation 23" also appear on a single (1978 MCA MCA-360, UK). "Variation 23/Variation 5" appear on a single (1978 MCA MCA-376, UK) and "Variation 23" appears on a single (1978 MCA PSR-423, UK).

LOVE SCULPTURE, DAVE EDMUNDS AND

244 ADD "DAVE EDMUNDS AND" TO NAME OF GROUP AS SHOWN ABOVE.

ADD AT END OF NOTE:
and on _Singles A's and B's_ (1980 Harvest SHSM-2032, UK) and on _Love Sculpture years, vol. 1_ (1987 Harvest EMS-1127, UK).

245 ADD AT END OF NOTE:
and on _Singles A's and B's_ (1980 Harvest SHSM-2032, UK). It is also included on the compilations _Wipeout--20 instrumental greats_ (1986 Impression LPIMP-5, UK) and _20 one hit wonders, vol. 1_ (1986 See for Miles CM-111, UK) and on _Love Sculpture years, vol. 1_ (1987 Harvest EMS-1127, UK).

MANN, MANFRED, 'S EARTH BAND

248 ADD UK ALBUM INFORMATION:
/ 1975 RSO 2479-167, UK.

ADD RELEVANT CONTENTS:
Relevant contents (segments credited to Prokofiev): Peter's theme -- Cat dance -- Cat -- Wolf -- Capture of wolf -- Duck escape -- Final theme

249 ADD AT END OF NOTE:
An updated version of "Joybringer" appears on the album _Masque_ (1987 10 Records DIX-69, UK).

MURPHEY, MICHAEL

255 REVISE NOTE:
Note: The alleged Scriabin piece occurs as a piano introduction and closing on the album version only.

MURPHY, WALTER

256 REVISE _WALTER MURPHY'S DISCOSYMPHONY_ ALBUM NUMBER PREFIX ON ENTRIES 256, 257, 262, 263 AND 269 TO READ: BXL1

263 ADD SOURCE INFORMATION:
Source: Mozart/Symphony no. 40 in G minor, K. 550

NEW LONDON CHORALE

275 ADD AT END OF NOTE:
This album was reissued (1985 RCA PL-70222, UK). Another version by various other artists was released (1990 Word 75021-8475-2, US [CD]).

NICE

299 ADD AT END OF NOTE:
and on The collection (1986 Castle CCSLP-106, UK).

300 ADD AT END OF NOTE:
The five bridges was reissued (1987 Mercury 422-830-291-1-M-1, US/ 1986 Charisma CHC-30, UK).

301 ADD AT END OF NOTE:
and on The collection (1986 Castle CCSLP-106, UK).

302 ADD AT END OF NOTE:
The five bridges was reissued (1987 Mercury 422-830-291-1-M-1, US/ 1986 Charisma CHC-30, UK).

303 ADD AT END OF NOTE:
and on The collection (1986 Castle CCSLP-106, UK).

304 ADD AT END OF NOTE:
Elegy was reissued (1987 Mercury 422-830-292-1-M-1, US/ 1986 Charisma CHC-1, UK).

NYLONS

308 ADD US ALBUM INFORMATION:
/ 1984 Open Air OA-0302, US.

PARKS, VAN DYKE

309 ADD NOTE:
Note: This album was reissued (1986 Edsel ED-213, UK).

PHILHARMONIC 2000

318 REVISE LABEL:
Phonogram = Philips

REPLACE CONTENTS AND SOURCES:
Contents and Sources: Disconcerto (Tchaikovsky/Piano concerto no. 1) -- Swan song (Tchaikovsky/Dance of the little swans) -- G-string boogie (J. S. Bach/Air from suite no. 3) -- Paradise lost (Borodin/ Polovetsian dances) -- Hallelujah hustle (Handel/ Hallelujah chorus) -- 1812/76 (Tchaikovsky/ 1812 overture) -- New world (Dvorák/New world symphony) -- Moonshine (Debussy/Clair de lune) -- Bees knees (Rimsky-Korsakov/Flight of the bumblebee)

-- Song and dance (Wagner/Tannhäuser overture) -- Big apple (Rossini/William Tell overture)

PILTDOWN MEN

319 ADD AT END OF NOTE:
and appears on the compilation _The Piltdown Men_ (1981 Capitol 054-82004, UK and Holland).

PRESLEY, ELVIS

320 ADD AT END OF NOTE:
also on _The alternate aloha_ (1988 RCA 6985-1-R8, US).

PROCOL HARUM

324 ADD PREFIX TO ALBUM NUMBER:
DES-

ADD UK HSAS ALBUM INFORMATION AND OTHER VERSIONS AT END OF NOTE:
/ 1984 Geffen GEF-25893, UK); Box Tops (_The Box Tops super hits_ 1968? Bell BELL-6025, US); David Lanz (_Cristofori's dream_ 1988 Narada Lotus ND-61021, US [album]; 1988 Narada Lotus N-53378, US [single]) which features Procol Harum organist Matthew Fisher; and Doro (Pesch) with Warlock (_Force majeure_ 1989 Mercury 838-016-1, US/ 1989 Vertigo 838-016-1, UK).

RAINBOW

332 ADD AT END OF NOTE:
The videocassette _Live between the eyes_ (1983 RCA/Columbia Musicvision 20282 [Beta]/60282 [VHS]/83052 [videodisc], US) includes "Difficult to cure." A live version of this piece backed by an orchestra appears on _Finyl vinyl_ (1986 Mercury 827-987-1-M-2, US/ 1986 Polydor PODV-8, UK). Videocassettes _Japan tour '84_ (1986 Polygram) and _The final cut_ (1986 RCA/Columbia Pictures Home Video) also include this live version with the orchestra.

RENAISSANCE

333 REVISE YEAR FOR ALBUM _IN THE BEGINNING_:
197? = 1978

RENAISSANCE ORCHESTRAL (ADD "L" TO ORCHESTRA)

334 ADD CONTENTS AND SOURCES AS LISTED ON ALBUM:
Contents: Farandole from L'Arlesienne suite (Bizet) -- Waltz in C sharp minor (Chopin) -- Bourée from water music (Handel) -- Jesu, joy of man's desiring (J. S. Bach) -- Anitra's dance from Peer Gynt suite (Grieg) -- Eine kleine nachtmusik, mvt. 1 from

Serenade in G (Mozart) -- Chinese dance from the Nutcracker suite (Tchaikovsky) -- Piano concerto no. 5 (Beethoven) -- 4th symphony, 3rd movement (Dvorák)

REVERE, PAUL AND THE RAIDERS

335 REVISE SOURCE INFORMATION:
Source: Rachmaninoff/Prelude in C sharp minor, op. 3, no. 2

ADD AT END OF NOTE:
It also appears on the compilation The legend of Paul Revere (1990 Columbia C2K-45311, US [CD]).

RIOS, WALDO DE LOS

337 REPLACE NOTE:
Note: The Manuel de Falla Orchestra, arranged and conducted by Waldo de los Rios, and its modern rhythm section perform: Mozart's 13th - Serenade no. 13 in G Major "Night of music" (Eine kleine nachtmusik K. 525) Allegro, Andante, Menuetto, Rondo -- What is love (Aria from The marriage of Figaro K. 492) -- Overture 492 (The marriage of Figaro K. 492) -- Mozart 21 (Concerto no. 21 for piano and orchestra in C major K. 467, 2nd mvt. "Andante") -- Musical charade (Musikalischer spass, 4th tempo "Presto") -- Mozart nova (variations on the theme "Dear harmony" from The magic flute)

ROYAL PHILHARMONIC ORCHESTRA

347 ADD AT END OF NOTE:
This album was nominated for 1981 and 1982 Grammy category of pop instrumental.

348 ADD UK ALBUM INFORMATION:
/ 1982 K-tel ONE-1173, UK.

349 ADD UK ALBUM INFORMATION:
/ 1983 K-tel ONE-1226, UK.

ADD AT END OF NOTE:
Selections of all three albums above are found on: The best of Hooked on classics (1983 K-tel ONE-1266, UK), Great hits from Hooked on classics (1984 Hallmark SHM-3158, UK) and The Hooked on classics collection (1989 K-tel 247-2, US [CD]/ 1988 K-tel ONCD-5107, UK [CD]).

SKY

(see also ADDENDA page 74 in 1985 discography)

358 ADD NOTE:
Note: This piece is also found on the compilation

Masterpieces: the very best of Sky (1984 Telstar STAR-2241, UK). Sky's first three albums are available as a box set Sky (1981 Ariola SKYBX-1, UK).

360 ADD NOTE:
Note: This piece is also found on the compilation Masterpieces: the very best of Sky (1984 Telstar STAR-2241, UK).

364 ADD AT END OF NOTE:
This piece is also found on the compilation Masterpieces: the very best of Sky (1984 Telstar STAR-2241, UK).

365 ADD AT END OF NOTE:
This piece is also found on the compilation Masterpieces: the very best of Sky (1984 Telstar STAR-2241, UK).

TEMPLE CITY KAZOO ORCHESTRA

380 ADD AT END OF NOTE:
This single was used in the film 16 candles (1984).

381 ADD NOTE:
Note: This piece also appears on the compilation The Rhino Brothers' greatest flops (1978-1985) (1986 Rhino RNLP-70827, US/ 198? Rhino/IMS RNLP-70827, UK).

TOMITA (Isao Tomita)

(see also ADDENDA page 74 in 1985 discography)

383 ADD AT END OF NOTE:
This album was reissued with the numbers ATL1-4332 and ARP1-4587.

385 ADD AT END OF NOTE:
and on The best of Tomita (198? RCA PD-89381, UK [CD]) and Tomita's greatest hits CD (1986 RCA Red Seal 5660-2-RC, US [CD]).

386 ADD AT END OF NOTE:
and on The best of Tomita (198? RCA PD-89381, UK [CD]) and Tomita's greatest hits CD (1986 RCA Red Seal 5660-2-RC, US [CD]).

387 ADD AT END OF NOTE:
A live version of "General dance" appears on The mind of the universe: live at Linz 1984 (1985 RCA Red Seal ARL1-5461, US/ 1985 RCA RL-85461, UK).

388 ADD AT END OF NOTE:
This piece appears as "The orb of beauty" on Space walk: impressions of an astronaut (1984 RCA Red Seal ARL1-5037, US/ 1984 RCA PL-85037, UK).

390 ADD NOTE:
Note: This piece appears as "Survival through technology" on _Space walk: impressions of an astronaut_ (1984 RCA Red Seal ARL1-5037, US/ 1984 RCA PL-85037, UK).

391 ADD NOTE:
Note: This piece appears as "No sound in space" on _Space walk: impressions of an astronaut_ (1984 RCA Red Seal ARL1-5037, US/ 1984 RCA PL-85037, UK). A live version of "The engulfed cathedral" appears on _Tomita live in New York - Back to the earth_ (1988 RCA Victor Red Seal 7717-1-RC, US).

392 REVISE NOTE BEGINNING WITH THIRD SENTENCE:
"Firebird: infernal dance" appears on _Tomita's greatest hits_ (1979 RCA Red Seal ARL1-3439, US/ 1979 RCA RL-43076, 1981 RCA RCALP-3037, UK), as "Infernal dance of King Kastchei" on _The best of Tomita_ (198? RCA PD-89381, UK [CD]) and on _Tomita's greatest hits CD_ (1986 RCA Red Seal 5660-2-RC, US [CD]). "Firebird suite: finale" appears on _A voyage through his greatest hits, vol. 2_ (1981 RCA Red Seal ARL1-4019, US) and live versions on _The mind of the universe: live at Linz 1984_ (1985 RCA Red Seal ARL1-5461, US/ 1985 RCA RL-85461, UK) and _Tomita live in New York - Back to the earth_ (1988 RCA Victor Red Seal 7717-1-RC, US).

393 REVISE SONG TITLE:
"Footprints in the snow."

ADD NOTE:
Note: This piece appears as "The orderly beauty of space" on _Space walk: impressions of an astronaut_ (1984 RCA Red Seal ARL1-5037, US/ 1984 RCA PL-85037, UK).

396 ADD AT END OF NOTE:
and on _The best of Tomita_ (198? RCA PD-89381, UK [CD]).

397 ADD AT END OF NOTE:
and on _The best of Tomita_ (198? RCA PD-89381, UK [CD]) and _Tomita's greatest hits CD_ (1986 RCA Red Seal 5660-2-RC, US [CD]).

398 ADD AT END OF NOTE:
"Grand Canyon suite: Sunrise" appears as "Opening the hatch" on _Space walk: impressions of an astronaut_ (1984 RCA Red Seal ARL1-5037, US/ 1984 RCA PL-85037, UK). "Grand Canyon suite: On the trail" also appears on _Tomita's greatest hits CD_ (1986 RCA Red Seal 5660-2-RC, US [CD]).

400 ADD AT END OF NOTE:
and on Tomita's greatest hits CD (1986 RCA RED SEAL 5660-2-RC, US [CD]).

401 ADD AT END OF NOTE:
"The fairy garden" appears as "Floating free" and "Pavan of the sleeping beauty" as "Thoughts of home" on Space walk: impressions of an astronaut (1984 RCA Red Seal ARL1-5037, US/ 1984 RCA PL-85037, UK).

402 ADD NOTE:
Note: This piece also appears on The best of Tomita (198? RCA PD-89381, UK [CD]).

405 ADD NOTE:
Note: This piece also appears on The best of Tomita (198? RCA PD-89381, UK [CD]).

407 ADD AT END OF NOTE:
and on Tomita's greatest hits CD (1986 RCA Red Seal 5660-2-RC, US [CD]). "Promenade" and "The old castle" also appear on The best of Tomita (198? RCA PD-89381, UK [CD]). "Tuileries" appears as "Coordinated activity," "Limoges" as "Get to work," and "The gnome" as "Leaving the ship" on Space walk: impressions of an astronaut (1984 RCA Red Seal ARL1-5037, US/ 1984 RCA PL-85037, UK).

408 ADD TO END OF SENTENCE BEFORE THE LAST SENTENCE IN NOTE:
and on Tomita's greatest hits CD (1986 RCA Red Seal 5660-2-RC, US [CD]).

ADD AT END OF NOTE:
The album reached #67 on the Billboard pop album chart and #1 on the classical chart. Live versions of "Jupiter," "Mars" and "Saturn" appear on The mind of the universe: live at Linz 1984 (1985 RCA Red Seal ARL1-5461, US/ 1985 RCA RL-85461, UK) and live versions of "Mars" and "Jupiter" also appear on Tomita live in New York - Back to the earth (1988 RCA Victor Red Seal 7717-1-RC, US).

410 ADD AT END OF NOTE:
and on The best of Tomita (198? RCA PD-89381, UK [CD]).

411 ADD AT END OF NOTE:
A live version titled "Three-part invention no. 2 in C minor" appears on Tomita live in New York - Back to the earth (1988 RCA Victor Red Seal 7717-1-RC, US).

412 ADD NOTE:
Note: This piece also appears on The best of Tomita (198? RCA PD-89381, UK [CD]). It appears as "Somersaults in space" on Space walk: impressions of

an astronaut (1984 RCA Red Seal ARL1-5037, US/ 1984 RCA PL-85037, UK).

413 ADD NOTE:
Note: A live version appears as "Violin concerto no. 1: moderato; allegro moderato" on The mind of the universe: live at Linz 1984 (1985 RCA Red Seal ARL1-5461, US/ 1985 RCA RL-85461, UK).

414 ADD AT END OF NOTE:
and on Tomita's greatest hits CD (1986 RCA Red Seal 5660-2-RC, US [CD]).

416 ADD NOTE:
Note: This piece also appears on Space walk: impressions of an astronaut (1984 RCA Red Seal ARL1-5037, US/ 1984 RCA PL-85037, UK).

417 ADD NOTE:
Note: This piece appears as "Fantasies of science fiction: Scythian suite: The adoration of Veles and Ala" on Space walk: impressions of an astronaut (1984 RCA Red Seal ARL1-5037, US/ 1984 RCA PL-85037, UK).

418 ADD NOTE:
Note: This piece appears as "Unsettling peace" on Space walk: impressions of an astronaut (1984 RCA Red Seal ARL1-5037, US/ 1984 RCA PL-85037, UK).

TYMES

424 ADD US ALBUM INFORMATION:
Somewhere. 1962 Parkway P-7039, US (album).

VALENS, RITCHIE

425 REVISE NOTE:
Note: This instrumental also appears on The best of Ritchie Valens (1981 Rhino RNDF-200, 1986 Rhino RNLP-70178, US) and on Ritchie Valens (a.k.a. Greatest hits or Memorial album) (1963 Del-Fi DFLP-1225, US). Ritchie Valens in concert at Pacoima Jr. High was reissued (1987 Rhino RNLP-70233, US).

WAKEMAN, RICK

441 REVISE SOURCE INFORMATION:
Source: Liszt/Dante sonata (symphony?)

ADD AT END OF NOTE:
A videocassette of the film Lisztomania (1981 Warner Home Video 11117, US) was released.

WONDER, STEVIE

458 REVISE UK ALBUM INFORMATION IN ENTRY:
1968 Tamla TML-11085 (mono), STML-11085 (stereo), UK.

ZAPPA, FRANK

465 REVISE US ALBUM INFORMATION IN ENTRY:
V-5013 (mono), V6-5013 (stereo)

REVISE US ALBUM INFORMATION IN NOTE:
V-5068 (mono), V6-5068 (stereo)

466 REVISE US ALBUM INFORMATION IN ENTRY:
V-5013 (mono), V6-5013 (stereo)

REVISE US ALBUM INFORMATION IN NOTE:
V-5068 (mono), V6-5068 (stereo)

467 REVISE US ALBUM INFORMATION IN ENTRY:
V-5055 (mono), V6-5055 (stereo)

468 REVISE US ALBUM INFORMATION IN ENTRY:
V-5013 (mono), V6-5013 (stereo)

REVISE US ALBUM INFORMATION IN NOTE:
V-5068 (mono), V6-5068 (stereo)

469 REVISE US ALBUM INFORMATION IN ENTRY:
V-8741 (mono), V6-8741 (stereo)

ADDENDA:

RESIDENTS

469A ADD UK ALBUM INFORMATION:
/ 1984 Korova KODE-9, UK.

McLAREN, MALCOLM

469B DELETE ENTIRE ENTRY--RELOCATED IN SUPPLEMENT (NEW ENTRIES, PART I).

TOMITA (Isao Tomita)

469D DELETE ENTIRE ENTRY--RELOCATED IN SUPPLEMENT (NEW ENTRIES, PART I).

469E DELETE ENTIRE ENTRY--RELOCATED IN SUPPLEMENT (NEW ENTRIES, PART I).

SKY

469G ADD NOTE:
Note: This piece is also found on the compilation Masterpieces: the very best of Sky (1984 Telstar STAR-2241, UK).

DEODATO (Eumir Deodato)

469H ADD AT END OF NOTE:
This piece also appears on Live at Felt Forum (1989 CBS Associated ZK45221, US [CD]).

II.
CLASSICIZIN' THE ROCK

ARANBEE POP SYMPHONY ORCHESTRA

470 ADD AT END OF NOTE:
This album was reissued as Pop symphony (1988 C5 522, UK).

BEATLES CRACKER SUITE

474 ADD AT END OF NOTE:
Conflicting reports in regard to this recording indicate the person responsible is either Fritz Spiegl or Arthur Wilkinson.

BEL-AIRE POPS ORCHESTRA

475 REVISE PREFIX FOR MONO ALBUM:
1965 Liberty LRP-3414 (mono), LST-7414 (stereo), US.

ADD CONTENTS:
Contents: The little old lady from Pasadena -- Baby talk -- Honolulu Lulu -- Dead man's curve -- Surf city -- It's a shame to say goodbye -- Drag city -- You really know how to hurt a guy -- Sidewalk surfin' -- Heart and soul -- The new girl in school -- Linda

FAITH, PERCY, ORCHESTRA/STRINGS

482 CHANGE (STRINGS) TO /STRINGS.

FANTABULOUS STRINGS

484 ADD PREFIXES:
M-557 (mono), MS-557 (stereo)

485 ADD PREFIXES:
M-554 (mono), MS-554 (stereo)

HOLLYRIDGE STRINGS

495 ADD AT END OF NOTE:
The flip side of this single is "Love me do."

497 REVISE MONO ALBUM NUMBER AND ADD NOTE:
1967 Capitol T-2656 (mono), ST-2656 (stereo), US.

Note: This album is sometimes called _Strawberry fields forever_.

502 ADD CONTENTS:
Contents: Mrs. Robinson -- Scarborough fair/Canticle -- The 59th Street Bridge song (Feelin' groovy) -- Homeward bound -- The sounds of silence -- I am a rock -- A hazy shade of winter -- The dangling conversation -- A most peculiar man -- Fakin' it -- At the zoo

KING'S SINGERS

504 ADD AT END OF NOTE:
"Life on Mars?" also appears on the compilations _For your pleasure_ (1983? Music for Pleasure MFP-5585, UK) and _This is the King's Singers_ (198? EMI THIS-9, UK).

505 ADD AT END OF NOTE:
"Morning has broken" also appears on the compilation _For your pleasure_ (1983? Music for Pleasure MFP-5585, UK.)

506 ADD AT END OF NOTE:
and on _Live at the Royal Festival Hall_ (1986 EMI EX290959-3, UK). "Ob-la-di, ob-la-da" also appears on the compilation _For your pleasure_ (1983? Music for Pleasure MFP-5585, UK). "I am a train" and "After the gold rush" also appear on _This is the King's Singers_ (198? EMI THIS-9, UK).

507 REVISE NOTE, LINE 2:
appaer = appear

508 ADD NOTE:
Note: "The fool on the hill" also appears on the compilation _For your pleasure_ (1983? Music for Pleasure MFP-5585, UK).

509 ADD AT END OF NOTE:
"Strawberry Fields forever" also appears on the compilations _For your pleasure_ (1983? Music for Pleasure MFP-5585, UK) and _This is the King's Singers_ (198? EMI THIS-9, UK).

KNIGHT, PETER, AND HIS ORCHESTRA

510 REVISE ENTRY AND ADD CONTENTS:
Sgt. Pepper's Lonely Hearts Club Band. 1967 Mercury MG-21132 (mono), SR-61132 (stereo), US.

Contents: Sgt. Pepper's Lonely Hearts Club Band -- With a little help from my friends -- Lucy in the sky with diamonds -- Getting better -- She's leaving home -- Within you without you -- When I'm sixty-four -- Lovely Rita -- Good morning good morning -- Sgt. Pepper's Lonely Hearts Club Band (reprise) -- A day in the life

LIVERPOOL STRINGS

513 ADD DATE, PREFIX AND COUNTRY:
1965? Metro M-560 (mono), MS-560 (stereo), US.

ADD CONTENTS:
Contents: I'm Henry VIII, I am -- Silhouettes -- Can't you hear my heartbeat -- Wonderful world -- I'm into something good -- Mrs. Brown you've got a lovely daughter -- Mother-in-law -- Show me a girl -- Sea cruise -- For your love

LIVING STRINGS

515 ADD CONTENTS AND NOTE:
Relevant contents: Hey Jude
Note: This album is also known by the title Songs made famous by the Beatles.

516 REVISE ALBUM NUMBER AND ADD CONTENTS:
1967 RCA Camden CAL-2148 (mono), CAS-2148 (stereo), US.

Contents: The Monkees -- (I'm not your) Steppin' stone -- When love comes knockin' (at your door) -- Last train to Clarksville -- I wanna be free -- The kind of girl I could love -- Take a giant step -- Mary, Mary -- She -- I'm a believer

518 ADD PREFIX TO ALBUM NUMBER AND ADD RELEVANT CONTENTS:
CAS-

Relevant contents: Aquarius (Fifth Dimension) -- Hey Jude (Beatles) -- Somethin' stupid (Nancy Sinatra) -- Blue velvet (Bobby Vinton)

LONDON PHILHARMONIC ORCHESTRA

526 DELETE ENTIRE ENTRY--RELOCATED IN SUPPLEMENT (NEW ENTRIES, PART I).

LONDON SYMPHONY ORCHESTRA

528 ADD UK ALBUM INFORMATION:
/ 1977 K-tel ONE-1009, UK.

ADD AT END OF NOTE:
This album was reissued (1987 Telescope STAR-6001, UK). The CD Classic rock (1987 JCI JCD-5251, US) includes the same selections and adds "Life on Mars?" (David Bowie) and "Sailing" (Christopher Cross).

529 ADD AT END OF NOTE:
This album was reissued (198? RCA AYL1-5027, US/ 1987 Telescope STAR-6002, UK).

530 ADD AT END OF NOTE:
This album was reissued (1987 Telescope STAR-6003, UK).

532 ADD AT END OF NOTE:
"Sad Jane" and "Mo 'n Herb's vacation I, II, and III" also appear on Zappa (1986 Rykodisc RCD-10022, US [CD]). A new version of "Bogus pomp" also appears on this CD.

533 REVISE ENTRY AND ADD CONTENTS:
Zappa, vol. II. 1987 Barking Pumpkin SJ-74207, US.

Contents: Bogus pomp -- Bob in dacron -- Strictly genteel

MANHATTAN STRINGS

534 ADD CONTENTS:
Contents: I'm a believer -- The day we fall in love -- I'm not your stepping stone -- Look out here comes tomorrow -- I wanna be free -- Last train to Clarksville -- She -- Theme from the Monkees -- Mary Mary -- Your Auntie Grizelda

MARTIN, GEORGE, ORCHESTRA

536 ADD US MONO ALBUM NUMBER IN NOTE:
1968 United Artists UAL-3647 (mono), UAS-6647 (stereo), US.

537 ADD US MONO ALBUM NUMBER IN ENTRY:
1965 United Artists UAL-3420 (mono), UAS-6420 (stereo), US.

540 ADD AT END OF NOTE:
This album was reissued (1988 C5 519, UK).

MAURIAT, PAUL, ORCHESTRA

542 ADD PARENTHESES ON CONTENTS:
(There's a) Kind of hush

ADD NOTE:
Note: ("There's a) Kind of hush" is also available on a single (1963 Parkway 891, US).

METROPOLITAN POPS ORCHESTRA

544 ADD NOTE:
Note: An alternate album title is _Instrumental versions of Bob Dylan favorites_.

545 ADD CONTENTS AND NOTE:
Contents: The cruel war -- Lemon tree -- All my trials -- Puff, the magic dragon -- If I had a hammer -- Man of constant sorrow -- Go tell it on the mountain -- 500 miles -- Blowin' in the wind
Note: An alternate album title is _Instrumental versions of Peter, Paul and Mary favorites_.

NITZSCHE, JACK, AND ORCHESTRA

549 ADD CONTENTS:
Contents: I want to hold your hand -- She loves you -- Chains -- My Bonnie -- I saw her standing there -- Ringo -- Please, please me -- From me to you -- All my loving -- Twist and shout -- It won't be long -- Beatle-mania

OLDHAM, ANDREW, ORCHESTRA

550 REVISE ENTRY:
1966 London LL-3457 (mono), PS-457 (stereo), US.

ADD AT END OF NOTE:
This album was reissued (198? Decca DOA-9, UK).

551 REVISE RELEVANT CONTENTS AFTER "LA BAMBA":
(Ritchie Valens; Tokens)

REVISE RELEVANT CONTENTS AT "MEMPHIS" TO:
Memphis, Tennessee (Chuck Berry)

ADD AT END OF NOTE:
Selected pieces from _The Rolling Stones songbook_ and _16 hip hits_ are also found on _Rarities_ (198? See For Miles SEE-36, UK; 1988 C5 518, UK).

101 STRINGS

554 REVISE ALBUM RELEASE DATE:
197? = 1972

555 REVISE ENTRY:
1977 Alshire S-5348, US.

560 REVISE ALBUM NUMBER TO READ:
S-5329

561 REVISE ALBUM RELEASE DATE AND ADD RELEVANT CONTENTS:
1972

Relevant contents: You can't hurry love (Supremes) -- Where did our love go (Supremes) -- Oh happy day (Edwin Hawkins Singers) -- Baby, let's smooth it over (Supremes)

562 REVISE ENTRY:
1981 Alshire S-5380, US.

PAGE, LARRY, ORCHESTRA

563 ADD AT END OF NOTE:
and as a picture-disc (1983 Rhino RNDF-257, US). A British reissue (1988 C5 521, UK) was also released.

RIFKIN, JOSHUA

571 ADD US MONO ALBUM NUMBER IN ENTRY:
1965 Elektra EKL-306 (mono), EKS-7306 (stereo), US.

REVISE ALBUM CONTENTS:
overture = ouverture
ADD BEFORE "TICKET TO RIDE": 5) Les plaisirs -
joking = jorking

ROCKIN' STRINGS

572 DELETE ENTRY BECAUSE CONTENTS REVEAL THAT THE SONGS INCLUDED ON THIS ALBUM WERE ORIGINALLY PERFORMED BY PRE-ROCK POP ARTISTS OF THE 1950s.

ROYAL LIVERPOOL PHILHARMONIC ORCHESTRA

574 REVISE LABEL AND ADD UK ALBUM INFORMATION:
MMG = Moss Music Group

/ 1979 Parlophone PAS-10014, UK.

ADD AT END OF NOTE:
A single was released which featured excerpts from The Beatles concerto titled "2nd movement: Andante espressivo/3rd movement: Presto" (1979 Parlophone R-6024, UK).

ROYAL PHILHARMONIC ORCHESTRA

575 ADD NOTE:
Note: The overture includes "Regatta de blanc/Spirits in the material world/Be my girl/ De do do do/Every little thing she does is magic/Regatta de blanc." In the US this album is available as a CD (1986 Dunhill DZS-002, US).

577 ADD TO RELEVANT CONTENTS:
-- Up where we belong (Joe Cocker and Jennifer Warnes)

578 REVISE ALBUM RELEASE DATE:
c1982, 1983

ADD CONTENTS:
Contents: All you need is love -- Hard day's night -- I want to hold your hand -- Here, there, and everywhere/Norwegian wood -- Fool on the hill -- Beatles medley -- Imagine (John Lennon) -- Blackbird -- Mull of Kintyre (Paul McCartney) -- Happy Xmas (War is over) (John Lennon) -- Sgt. Pepper medley

ADD NOTE:
Note: The Royal Choral Society joins the Royal Philharmonic Orchestra with Louis Clark, conductor. The album was recorded December 13, 1982 at Royal Albert Hall in London. In the US this album is available on CD (1986 Dunhill DZS-001, US). A videocassette <u>An orchestral tribute to the Beatles</u> was released (1987 Sony Video R0591, US).

579 ADD AT END OF NOTE:
A CD was released titled <u>Classically Queen</u> (1987 Prism Entertainment CD-203, US).

SPIEGL, FRITZ

581 REVISE SPELLING OF SPIEGEL IN ENTRY AND NOTE:
change Spiegel to Spiegl

REVISE ALBUM RELEASE DATE TO READ:
1965

ADDENDA:

BOULEZ, PIERRE

584B ADD UK ALBUM INFORMATION AND ADD CONTENTS:
/ 1985 EMI EL270153-1, UK

Contents: The perfect stranger -- Naval aviation in art? -- The girl in the magnesium dress -- Outside now, again -- Love story -- Dupree's paradise -- Jonestown

III.
OTHER CONNECTIONS BETWEEN ROCK AND THE CLASSICS

A. Rock Groups or Artists Recording with Established Orchestras and Choruses

DEEP PURPLE

594 ADD AT END OF NOTE:
A videocassette was later released (1984 BBC, UK).

EMERSON, LAKE & PALMER

597 ADD AT END OF NOTE:
A 1981 videocassette with the same title was released in Canada.

ENO, BRIAN

601 ADD SONG TITLE:
"Put a straw under baby."

LORD, JON

603 ADD AT END OF NOTE:
The album was reissued (1984 Safari LONG-10, UK).

605 REVISE B# IN CONTENTS TO B NATURAL.

NICE

610 ADD AT END OF NOTE:
The five bridges was reissued (1987 Mercury 422-830-291-1-M-1, US/ 1986 Charisma CHC-30, UK).

OLDFIELD, MIKE

612 ADD AT END OF NOTE:
This album was reissued (198? Virgin OVED-97, UK).

PARSONS, ALAN, PROJECT

617 ADD AT END OF NOTE:
A remixed and remastered version was released (1988 Mercury 832820-1, US/ 1988 Mercury LONLP-48, UK).

PINK FLOYD

621 ADD AT END OF NOTE:
A half-speed mastered version of this album was released (1983 Columbia H2C-46183, US). A live version of The wall live in Berlin (1990 Mercury/ Polygram 846-611-1, US and UK) was produced and performed by Roger Waters (formerly of Pink Floyd)

with his Bleeding Heart Band, the East Berlin Rundfunk (Radio) Orchestra & Choir, and many other guest artists. It was recorded July 21, 1990 at Potsdamer Platz in Berlin. Guest stars were Sinéad O'Connor, Joni Mitchell, Cyndi Lauper, Van Morrison, Thomas Dolby, Bryan Adams, Marianne Faithfull, Paul Carrack, Scorpions, The Band, Albert Finney, Tim Curry and James Galway. The music was orchestrated and conducted by Michael Kamen. This concert celebrated the removal of the Berlin Wall and was a benefit concert for the Memorial Fund for Disaster Relief. A videocassette The wall live in Berlin (1990 Polygram Music Video 082-649-3, US) was also released.

RONSTADT, LINDA

628 REPLACE LAST SENTENCE IN THE NOTE WITH:
This album reached #3 on the Billboard pop chart. A videocassette Linda Ronstadt (with Nelson Riddle and his Orchestra) in concert (1984 Vestron Video 1012, US) was released.

WAKEMAN, RICK

633 IN THE FIRST SENTENCE OF NOTE REPLACE THE PHRASE "A FORTY-FIVE PIECE STUDIO ORCHESTRA" WITH:
the New World Symphony Orchestra

WAYNE, JEFF

635 REVISE INFORMATION FOR ABRIDGED VERSION IN NOTE:
(1978 CBS 85337, US/ 1978 CBS CBS-32356, UK)

WHO

636 ADD UK ALBUM INFORMATION IN ENTRY:
; Polydor 2657-014, UK.

ADD TO CONTENTS BETWEEN "MIRACLE CURE" AND "SALLY SIMPSON":
Sensation

ADD AFTER RICHIE HAVENS IN NOTE:
(The Hawker)

637 DELETE PHRASE FROM CONTENTS:
"Sensation" is added

YOUNG, NEIL

638 ADD RELEASE DATE FOR REISSUE ALBUM 2277 IN ENTRIES 638 AND 639:
1977

ZAPPA, FRANK

640 ADD AT END OF NOTE:
A videocassette titled Frank Zappa's 200 Motels (1988 MGM/UA Home Video, US) was released.

C. Selected Examples of Rock music Simulating a Baroque or Classical Sound/Structure

ABC

677 ADD AT END OF NOTE:
"All of my heart"/"Overture" was also released separately (1982 Vertigo/Neutron SOUX-2317, UK [12" single]).

BEATLES

694 ADD ALBUM REISSUE INFORMATION AFTER NUMBERS LISTED IN ENTRIES 694, 696, AND 698:
5715 (6297)

696 5810 (6299)

698 5498 (6291)

BOOMTOWN RATS

703 ADD AT END OF NOTE:
and the compilation The best of the Boomtown Rats (1987 Columbia FC-40615, US).

CROSBY & NASH

717 ADD AT END OF NOTE:
Wind on the water was reissued (19?? MCA 37007; 198? MCA MCA-1581, US).

DOORS

720 ADD AFTER THE FIRST SENTENCE OF THE NOTE:
This song performed by the Doors and orchestrated with strings was televised on the Smothers Brothers Comedy Hour. A videocassette Dance on fire (1985 MCA Home Video VHS-80157, US) includes this performance.

ADD AT END OF NOTE:
This song is also included on a different compilation titled The best of the Doors (1987 Elektra 60345-1, US/ 1985 Elektra[USA] EKT-21, UK).

ELECTRIC LIGHT ORCHESTRA

724 ADD AT END OF NOTE:
"Can't get it out of my head" and "Boy blue" also

appear on the film soundtrack album Joyride (1977 United Artists UA-LA784-H, US).

725 ADD AT END OF NOTE:
This album was reissued (1984 Jet JET-32545, UK).

726 ADD AT END OF NOTE:
"Rockaria" also appears on the film soundtrack album Joyride (1977 United Artists UA-LA784-H, US).

727 ADD AT END OF NOTE:
"10538 overture" also appears on the compilation album The light shines on (1977 Harvest SHSM-2015, UK).

ELECTRIC PRUNES

728 REVISE US ALBUM INFORMATION:
1967 Reprise R-6275 (mono), RS-6275 (stereo), US/

FAITHFULL, MARIANNE

734 ADD AT END OF NOTE:
Greatest hits was reissued as The best of ... (1981 London MIP-1-9372, US) and again as Greatest hits (1987 Abkco 7547-1, US). A remake of this song appears on the album Strange weather (1987 Island 7-90613-1, US/ 1987 Island ILPS-9874, UK).

GENESIS

738 ADD AT END OF NOTE:
This album was reissued (1984 Charisma CHC-22, UK).

HARRIS, RICHARD

743 ADD AT END OF NOTE:
It won a 1968 Grammy for best arrangement accompanying a vocalist.

IT'S A BEAUTIFUL DAY

745 ADD AT END OF NOTE:
The album was reissued (197? San Francisco Sound SFS-11790, US/ 1980 CBS 83787, UK).

JOHN, ELTON

752 ADD TO NOTE AFTER ALBUM NUMBER MCA-3027:
(5225)

753 ADD TO NOTE AFTER ALBUM NUMBER MCA-3027:
(5225)

KANSAS

755 ADD AT END OF NOTE:
A half-speed mastered version was released (1981 Kirshner HZ-44224, US).

KING CRIMSON

758 ADD TO NOTE AFTER THE FIRST SENTENCE:
A reissue (198? Editions EG 2302-057, UK) was released.

759 ADD AT END OF NOTE:
A reissue (198? Editions EG 2302-060, UK) was released.

LED ZEPPELIN

761 REPLACE NOTE WITH:
A mellotron adds string-like sounds to this song.

LEFT BANKE

763 ADD AT END OF NOTE:
The song also appears on History of the Left Banke, 1966-73 (1985 Rhino RNLP-123, US).

764 ADD AT END OF NOTE:
The song also appears on History of the Left Banke, 1966-73 (1985 Rhino RNLP-123, US).

LITTLE RIVER BAND

768 ADD AT END OF NOTE:
A studio version of this song also appears on Greatest hits (1982 Capitol ST-12247, US). A live version performed with the Adelaide Symphony Orchestra appears on Backstage pass (1980 Capitol SWBK-12061, US).

LLOYD-WEBBER, ANDREW

769 ADD UK ALBUM INFORMATION TO ENTRY:
/ 1970 MCA/Decca MKPS-2011/2 (MAPS-2075/6), UK.

ADD TO NOTE AT END OF SECOND SENTENCE:
/ 1973 MCA MCX-501, UK). The original London cast stage version (1972 Decca MDKS-8008, UK) was reissued (1974 MCA MCF-2503, UK). A UK motion picture version was also released (1973 MCA/Decca MCX-502, UK).

ADD TO NOTE AT END OF THIRD SENTENCE AFTER "MCA2-11000, US":
/ 1973 MCA/Decca MCX-502, UK).

ADD ALTERNATE US BROADWAY VERSION ALBUM NUMBERS TO NOTE AFTER "1971 MCA DL7-1503":
; MCA-5000, US).

ADD UK SINGLE INFORMATION TO NOTE AFTER "I DON'T KNOW HOW TO LOVE HIM":
/ 1971 MCA/Decca MKS-5063, UK).

ADD AT END OF NOTE:
Another single was titled "Jesus Christ Superstar" (1969 MCA/Decca DCL-79 (178-79), US/ 1969 MCA MKS-5019, UK).

770 ADD UK ALBUM INFORMATION TO ENTRY:
/ 1969 Decca SKL-4973, UK.

ADD UK ALBUM INFORMATION TO NOTE AFTER US 1974 ALBUM INFORMATION:
/ 1974 MCA MCF-2544, UK).

ADD AT END OF NOTE:
This rock opera was also recorded as a new Broadway production (1982 Chrysalis FV-41387, US) and a British production (The Young Vic Production 1983 Polydor SPELP-6, UK).

LOVE UNLIMITED ORCHESTRA

771 ADD AT BEGINNING OF NOTE:
This instrumental originally appeared on Love Unlimited's <u>Under the influence of Love Unlimited</u> (1973 20th Century T-414, US).

ADD TO NOTE AFTER FIRST SENTENCE:
"Love's theme" also appears on Love Unlimited's <u>In heat</u> (1974 20th Century T-443, US).

MAURIAT, PAUL

773 REVISE ALBUM AND SINGLES RELEASE DATES:
1967

ADD AT BEGINNING OF NOTE:
Note: Mauriat's arrangement combines a rock beat with a chamber orchestra style.

MOODY BLUES

776 ADD AT END OF NOTE:
The album was reissued (1984 Deram DOA-7, UK).

777 ADD AT END OF NOTE:
The Moody Blues featured the mellotron on their albums. The mellotron is a keyboard instrument which employs tape loops of pre-recorded sound (e.g., strings) each for a specific note.

NICE

782 ADD AT END OF NOTE:
The suite also appears on The collection (1986 Castle CCSLP-106, UK).

ORCHESTRAL MANOEUVRES IN THE DARK

788 ADD AT END OF NOTE:
This piece also appears as "Maid of Orleans" on the compilation The best of OMD (1988 A&M SP-5186, US/ 1988 Virgin OMD-1, UK).

PARKS, VAN DYKE

791 ADD US MONO ALBUM NUMBER TO ENTRY:
1968 Warner Bros. W-1727 (mono), WS-1727 (stereo), US

ADD AT END OF NOTE:
This album was reissued (1986 Edsel ED-207, UK).

PHILLIPS, ANTHONY

794 ADD US ALBUM INFORMATION TO ENTRY AND REVISE UK ALBUM RELEASE DATE TO 1982:
1982 Passport PVC-8908, US/

795 ADD NOTE:
Note: This album was reissued (1982 Passport PVC-8905, US).

PINK FLOYD

797 REVISE "400 WEEKS" IN NOTE TO:
700 plus weeks

CLARIFY RELEASE DATE AND NUMBER FOR HALF-SPEED MASTERED ALBUM AT END OF NOTE:
197? Mobile MFSL-1-017, US).

ADD AT END OF NOTE:
A picture disc (1978 Capitol SEAX-11902, US) and an ultra high quality recording (1982 Mobile Fidelity Sound Lab MFQR-1-027, US) were released.

QUEEN

802 ADD TO NOTE AFTER FIRST SENTENCE:
It won the British Phonographic Society's 1975 award for best single of the previous 25 years.

ADD AT END OF NOTE:
and on Live magic (1986 Capitol ?, US/ 1986 EMI EMC-3519, UK).

RENAISSANCE

805 CLARIFY ALBUM RELEASE DATE IN NOTE:
197? = 1978

ROCKESTRA

806 ADD AT END OF NOTE:
"Rockestra theme" originally appeared on Wings' _Back to the egg_ (1979 Columbia FC-36057, US/ 1979 Parlophone 257, UK) with guitars by Pete Townshend, David Gilmour, Denny Laine, Lawrence Juber and bass by Paul McCartney, Bruce Thomas and Ronnie Lane. The piece won a 1979 Grammy for best instrumental recording. _Back to the egg_ is also available as a video album. The later version is also in the film _Rock for Kampuchea_ (1981).

RUSH

814 ADD AT END OF NOTE:
Sections of this piece also appear on the live album _All the world's a stage_ (1976 Mercury SRM-2-7508, US/ 1976 Mercury 6672-015, UK).

STEVENS, CAT

823 ADD AT END OF NOTE:
and also appears on the compilation _Footsteps in the dark: greatest hits volume two_ (1984 A&M SP-3736, US).

SUPREMES

831 ADD UK SINGLE INFORMATION:
/ 1965 Tamla Motown TMG-543, UK.

SYNERGY

834 ADD NOTE:
Note: This album was reissued (1979 Passport PB-6001, US).

TANGERINE DREAM

835 ADD NOTE:
Note: This album was reissued (1984 Virgin OVED-25, UK).

ULTRAVOX

843 ADD AT END OF NOTE:
Both "Hymn" and "Vienna" are also on _Monument: the soundtrack_ (1983 Chrysalis CUX-1452, UK) and _The collection_ (1985 Chrysalis FV-41490, US/ 1984 Chrysalis UTV-1, UK).

UNITED STATES OF AMERICA

844 REVISE US ALBUM NUMBER IN ENTRY TO READ: 9614

ADD AT END OF NOTE:
This album was reissued (1987 Edsel ED-233, UK).

WHO

851 ADD AT END OF NOTE:
A videocassette of the film _Tommy_ (1982 Columbia Pictures Home Entertainment VH10555E; 1987 RCA/Columbia Pictures Home Video 60245, US) was released. A special twentieth anniversary live performance of the rock opera _Tommy_ is featured on the triple album _Join together_ (1990 MCA MCA3-19501, US) and on the videocassette _The Who live: featuring the rock opera Tommy_ (1989 CBS Music Video Enterprises 19V-49028, US). A special 1989 benefit performance at the Universal Amphitheatre, Los Angeles featured the Who with guest artists, Phil Collins, Billy Idol, Elton John, Patti LaBelle and Steve Winwood.

WILLIAMS, MASON

853 ADD AT END OF NOTE:
It also won 1968 Grammys for best instrumental arrangement, best contemporary pop performance, and best instrumental theme. An updated version appears on Mason Williams & Mannheim Steamroller's _Classical gas_ (1987 American Gramaphone AG-800, US).

ZAPPA, FRANK

(see also Parts I and IIIA in 1985 discography)

862 ADD AT END OF NOTE:
"Bogus pomp" as recorded with the London Symphony Orchestra appears on _Zappa_ (1986 Rykodisc RCD-10022, US (CD)).

D. Rock Music Influences on Classical Music

1. Classical Composers

GLASS, PHILIP

868 ADD AT BEGINNING OF NOTE:
Act I of this album has text written by David Byrne.

2. Classical Record Packaging

FOX, VIRGIL

870 ADD AT END OF NOTE:
The album was reissued (198? MCA MCA-28, US).

871 ADD AT END OF NOTE:
The album was reissued (198? MCA MCA-42, US).

882 CORRECT APOSTROPHE:
Brahm's = Brahms'

ADD TO NOTE:
These albums were reissued in 1984 on the CBS Masterworks label numbers M-39431 through M-39455.

ADD TO LIST:
<u>Bernstein's greatest hits</u>. 1971 Columbia M-30304, US.

883 ADD TO LIST:
<u>Bernstein's greatest hits</u>. 1973 RCA Red Seal ARL1-0108, US.

3. Rock Artists Appearing in Straight Classical Roles

BOWIE, DAVID

891 ADD AT END OF NOTE:
The album reached #136 on the Billboard <u>pop</u> chart.

BYRNE, DAVID

892 DELETE THE WORD "ONLY" IN NOTE.

ADD TO NOTE AFTER THE WORD "CASSETTE":
and the CD <u>The complete score from the Catherine Wheel</u> (c1981, 1987 Sire 3645-2, US).

ADD TO NOTE AFTER "SRK-3645, US":
and UK).

ADD TO NOTE AFTER THIRD SENTENCE:
Excerpts were also released as <u>3 big songs: Songs from the Broadway production of the Catherine Wheel</u> (1981 Sire DSRE-50034, US [EP]). This work premièred September 22, 1981 at Winter Garden Theatre, New York City. A videocassette <u>The Catherine wheel</u> was released (1982 Thorn EMI/HBO Video TVE-3397, US).

<u>The civil wars</u>. <u>See also</u> entry 890 in 1985 discography and Supplement, Part IIID3, entry S520.

DALTREY, ROGER

893 ADD AT END OF NOTE:
A home videocassette Beggar's opera was released in 1983 by BBC Television (UK) and in 1985 by Home Vision (US). Both are distributed by NVC Arts International.

RONSTADT, LINDA

896 REVISE NOTE:
Ronstadt starred as Mabel in this recording of the 1981 Broadway production of Gilbert and Sullivan's operetta. A film of this production was released in 1983. A videocassette (1983 MCA Home Video VHS-71012, US) and a videodisc (1983 MCA Home Video MCA45-17011, US) were also released. The 1981 road company of "The Pirates of Penzance" featured Andy Gibb. A 1982 production featured Peter Noone (formerly of Herman's Hermits) as Frederic and Maureen McGovern as Mabel.

ADD CROSS REFERENCE:

ZAPPA, FRANK

See entries 532, 533 and 584B in 1985 discography. (Some selections on these albums were composed originally for orchestra.)

APPENDIX B. SELECTED JAZZ VERSIONS OF THE CLASSICS

Swingle Singers.
ADD MONO ALBUM NUMBERS: Anyone for Mozart? PHM-200-149
Bach's greatest hits. PHM-200-097
Getting romantic. PHM-200-191

REVISE YEAR OF RELEASE: Going baroque to 1964

APPENDIX C. SELECTED PARODIES OF THE CLASSICS

Jones, Spike.
REVISE YEAR FOR ALBUM DINNER MUSIC:
19?? = 1962?

Sherman, Allan.
ADD ALBUM INFORMATION:
My son, the nut. 1963 Warner Bros. W-1501, US (album);

APPENDIX D.
SELECTED COUNTRY AND FOLK VERSIONS OF THE CLASSICS

Kottke, Leo.

ADD AT BEGINNING OF NOTE FOR "JESU, JOY OF MAN'S DESIRING": This piece also appears on 6 & 12-string guitar (1972 Takoma C-1024, Takoma TAK-7024, US/ 1972 Sonet SNTF-629, Takoma TKMLP-6002, UK).

Appendix A.

Selected Big Band and Broadway Versions of the Classics

Broadway Shows that Borrowed Musical Themes from the Classics

Beggar's holiday (1946) John Gay
Carmen Jones (1943) Georges Bizet
The great waltz (1934) Johann Strauss
Helen goes to Troy (1944) Jacques Offenbach
Kismet (1953) Alexander Borodin
Music in my heart (1947) Peter Ilich Tchaikovsky
My darlin' Aida (1952) Giuseppe Verdi
Natja (1925) Peter Ilich Tchaikovsky
Three waltzes (1937) Johann Strauss I & II

Foreign Shows that Borrowed Musical Themes from the Classics

Bohème '86 (1986) Giacomo Puccini -- Vienna
Carmen Negra (1988) Georges Bizet -- Vienna
Figaro (198?) Wolfgang Amadeus Mozart -- London

Appendix B.

Selected Jazz and New Age Versions of the Classics

Barber, Billy. "Chopin etude no. 4." Lighthouse. 1986 DMP CD-455, US (CD).

Bedrosian, Wayne. Jazzical class (with Los Angeles Concert Trio). 1984 Perpetua PR-7003, US (CD). (Bach; Mozart)

Bedrosian, Wayne. Wayne Bedrosian and the London Symphony Orchestra performing jazzical class. 1987 Perpetua PR-7012, US (CD). (Tchaikovsky; Mozart)

Brady, Victor. Classical soul. 1976 Inner City IC-1006, US. (steel "piano")

Cantabile. "Air on the G string (Smoke gets in your throat)" (J. S. Bach); "Orpheus in the underground" (Offenbach); "The history of the world" (R. Strauss; Handel; J. S. Bach; Mozart; Beethoven; Tchaikovsky; Debussy). Hear no evil. 1983 Plant Life PLR-069, UK.

Cicero, Eugen. Classics in rhythm. 1988 Verve/MPS 817924-2, US (CD). (Bach; Mozart; Chopin; Tchaikovsky)

Coryell, Larry. Firebird/Petrushka. 1984 IMS/Philips 812-864-1, UK. (Stravinsky)

Coryell, Larry. Le sacre du printemps. 1983 Philips 814-750-1, UK. (Stravinsky)

Coryell, Larry. Scheherazade/Bolero. 198? Philips 810-024-1, UK. (Rimsky-Korsakov; Ravel)

Farmer, Art. Baroque sketches. 1966? Columbia CL-2588 (mono), US.

Fest, Manfredo. "Bach's prelude and fugue #2 (ala disco)." Manifestations. 1979 Tabu BL(JZ)-35636, US.

Glover, Bob. _Popped-up Bach and other classical lites_. 1988 New Age Music D2-72201, US (CD). (Pachelbel; Mozart; Bach; Boccherini; Schumann; Offenbach; Clarke; Chopin; Beethoven)

Hand, Frederic. _Baroque and on the street: Vivaldi favorites_. 1981 CBS FM-36687, US.

Hand, Frederic. _Jazzantiqua_. 1984 Musical Heritage Society MHS-4887, US. (1986 RCA Red Seal AML1-7126, US).

Hyman, Dick and Ruby Braff. "Swan Lake." _Fireworks_. 1985 Inner City IC-1153, US. (Tchaikovsky)

James, Bob. "Ludwig." _Foxie_. 1983 Columbia/Tappan Zee FC-38801, US/ 1983 CBS 25546, UK. (Beethoven)

James, Bob. _Rameau_. 1984 CBS Masterworks Digital IM-39540, US and UK.

James, Bob. _The Scarlatti dialogues_. 1988 CBS Masterworks M-44519, US.

Kingsley, Gershon. _Mozart after hours_. 1964 Vanguard VRS-9165 (mono), US.

Laws, Hubert. "Suite in A minor for flute and strings." _New earth sonata_. 1985 CBS Masterworks M-39858, US. (Telemann)

Laws, Hubert. "Ravel's Bolero." _Family_. 1980 Columbia JC-36396, US. (Ravel/Bolero)

Lewis, John. _The bridge game_. 1986 Philips 826-698-1, US and UK. (J. S. Bach/Preludes and Fugues from The well-tempered clavier, book I)

Lewis, John. _Preludes and fugues from The well-tempered clavier: book I_. 1985 Philips 824-381-1, US and UK. (J. S. Bach)

Loussier, Jacques. _Bach to the future_. 1986 Start STL-8, UK.

Loussier, Jacques. _Reflections of Bach_. 1987 Chrysalis FV-41591, US/ 1987 Start STL-9, UK.

101 Strings with All-Star Orchestra and pipe organ. _Scheherajazz: a symphony in jazz_. 1986 Alshire ALCD-15, US (CD). (Rimsky-Korsakov)

Sea Mailman. _Jazz arrangements of classics_. 1986 Denon C38-7686, UK (CD).

Slawson, Brian. _Bach on wood_. 1985 CBS M-39704, US.

Spiegelman, Joel. *New age Bach: the Goldberg variations*. 1988 East-West 7-90927-1, US.

Swingle Singers. *Anyone for Mozart, Bach, Handel, Vivaldi?*. 1986 Philips 826-948-1, US and UK. (compilation)

Swingle Singers. *Jazz Sebastian Bach*. 1985 Philips 824-544-1 and 824-703-1, US and UK. (compilation)

Tatum, Art. *Pure genius*. 1984 Affinity AFFD-118, UK. Relevant contents: Elegie (Massenet) -- Humoresque (Dvorák)

Tatum, Art. *Solos (1940)*. 1990 MCA MCA-42327, US. Relevant contents: Elegie (Massenet) -- Humoresque (Dvorák)

Valente, Caterina. *Classics with a chaser*. 1960 RCA Victor LSP-2119, US.

Various Artists. *Bach for a new age*. 1990 ProJazz CDJ-729, US (CD).

Various Artists. *Narada Nutcracker*. 1990 Narada ND-63904, US (CD). (Tchaikovsky)

Waller, Fats. "Ah! So pure." *Complete recordings, vol. 18*. 1939 RCA FXM1-7316, US. (Flowtow/Martha)

Waller, Fats. "My heart at thy sweet voice." *Complete recordings, vol. 19*. 1939-40 RCA PM-42027, US. (Saint-Saëns/Samson and Delilah)

Waller, Fats. "Sextet." *Complete recordings, vol. 19*. 1939-40 RCA PM-42027, US. (Donizetti/Lucia di Lammermoor)

Waller, Fats. "Then you'll remember me." *Complete recordings, vol. 19*. 1939-40 RCA PM-42027, US. (Balfe/The Bohemian girl)
Note: The above three pieces also appear on *Jazz anthology* (1939-40 RCA 30-JA-5148, US).

Appendix C.

Selected Parodies of the Classics

Jones, Spike. Spike Jones is murdering the classics. c1971 RCA Gold Seal AGL1-4142(e), US.
Note: This reissue of an earlier release adds "William Tell overture" and "Rhapsody from hunger(y)."

Portsmouth Sinfonia. Hallelujah. 1974 Antilles AN-7002, US.

Schickele, Peter (P.D.Q. Bach). 1712 overture and other musical assaults. 1989 Telarc Digital CD-80210, US (CD).

Appendix D. Selected Country and Folk Versions of the Classics

Baez, Joan. "Bachinanas Brasileiras - aria." Joan Baez 5. 1964 Vanguard VRS-9160 (mono), VSD-79160 (stereo); 1964 Fontana STFL-6043, US. (Villa-Lobos)

Bull, Sandy. "Fifth of brandy." Jukebox school of music. 1989 ROM, US. (J.S. Bach/Brandenburg concerto no. 5)

Campbell, Glen. "William Tell overture." 1977 Capitol 4376, US (single). B-side of "Southern nights." (Rossini)

Cole, B. J. Transparent music. 1989 Hannibal HNBL-1325, US and UK. (Ravel; Debussy)

Critton Hollow String Band. "Melody." Great dreams. 1989 Flying Fish FF-468, US. (Paganini)

Fahey, John. "Dvorák." Let go. 1984 Varrick VR-008, US.

Fahey, John. "Lullaby and finale." Rainforests, oceans, and other themes. 1986 Varrick VR-019, US. (Stravinsky/ Firebird)

Greene, Richard. "Bach violin concerto in E major (except 3rd movement)." Ramblin'. 1979 Rounder Records 0110, US.

Nelson, Willie. "Bach minuet in G." The promiseland. 1986 Columbia FC-40327, US/ 1986 CBS 26852, UK.

Orison. "The dance of the spirits of water/The golden goose." Orison. 1988 Gourd Music GM-104, US (CD). (Holst)

Prophet, Ronnie. "Phantom of the opry." Alive. 1984 Audiograph ADG 6023, US. (Bach/Toccata and fugue in D minor, BWV 538)

Steeleye Span. "The black freighter" and "The wife of the soldier." Storm force ten. 1977 Chrysalis CHR-1151, US and UK. (Weill/The threepenny opera)

Steeleye Span. "Cannon by Telemann." Back in line. 1986 Shanachie 79063, US. (Telemann)

Williamson, Robin. Winter's turning. 1986 Flying Fish FF-407, US. (Praetorius' courante; Vivaldi's winter largo; Corelli's sonato)

Index

Note: Numbers in this index refer to entry numbers. The general index covers rock artists, rock groups, orchestras, choruses, classical composers, producers, conductors, and song or instrumental titles. Album titles are not indexed. Certain songs and instrumentals are indexed by commonly known classical nicknames (e.g., "Flight of the bumblebee") if that is the title used on the recording, but not all such pieces based on the same theme have the same title. Therefore, the classical composer's name should be consulted in the index in order to locate <u>all</u> versions of the piece. Under the composer's name, some works have been sectioned out when they have been borrowed more often than the others, but generally the works are gathered together in one entry number sequence. Alphabetization is generally word by word. Mac and Mc are listed as spelled, not mixed. The names of rock groups and song/instrumental titles are listed alphabetically excluding initial English and foreign articles (i.e., a, an, the, l', la, les, eine, el, las, los). Number sequences after a common initial word or words are in numerical order. Abbreviations (e.g., Mr., no.) are listed as spelled. Acronyms are listed at the beginning of their respective alphabetical sections. Entries beginning with numerals are listed as if the numerals were spelled out in words. New entry numbers for this Supplement are preceded by the letter prefix "S". Part IV, "Update," entry numbers correspond to those in the 1985 discography and are preceded in the index by the word "Update" and a colon. This index is intended for use in tandem with the index of the 1985 discography in order to identify all related entries.

ABOUT THE COMPILER

JANELL R. DUXBURY is a Librarian in Central Technical Services-Humanities at the Memorial Library of the University of Wisconsin-Madison and author of the previous related book *Rockin' the Classics and Classicizin' the Rock: A Selectively Annotated Discography* (Greenwood Press, 1985).

www.ingramcontent.com/pod-product-compliance
Lightning Source LLC
Chambersburg PA
CBHW020401100426
42812CB00001B/145

9780313275425